Mastering Machine Learning for Penetration Testing

Develop an extensive skill set to break self-learning systems using Python

Chiheb Chebbi

BIRMINGHAM - MUMBAI

Mastering Machine Learning for Penetration Testing

Commissioning Editor: Vijin Boricha
Acquisition Editor: Heramb Bhavsar
Content Development Editor: Nithin George Varghese
Technical Editor: Komal Karne
Copy Editor: Safis Editing
Project Coordinator: Virginia Dias
Proofreader: Safis Editing
Indexer: Tejal Daruwale Soni
Graphics: Tom Scaria
Production Coordinator: Aparna Bhagat

First published: June 2018

Production reference: 1260618

Published by Packt Publishing Ltd.
Livery Place
35 Livery Street
Birmingham
B3 2PB, UK.

ISBN 978-1-78899-740-9

www.packtpub.com

I dedicate this book to every person who makes the security community awesome and fun!

`mapt.io`

Mapt is an online digital library that gives you full access to over 5,000 books and videos, as well as industry leading tools to help you plan your personal development and advance your career. For more information, please visit our website.

Why subscribe?

- Spend less time learning and more time coding with practical eBooks and Videos from over 4,000 industry professionals

- Improve your learning with Skill Plans built especially for you

- Get a free eBook or video every month

- Mapt is fully searchable

- Copy and paste, print, and bookmark content

PacktPub.com

Did you know that Packt offers eBook versions of every book published, with PDF and ePub files available? You can upgrade to the eBook version at `www.PacktPub.com` and as a print book customer, you are entitled to a discount on the eBook copy. Get in touch with us at `service@packtpub.com` for more details.

At `www.PacktPub.com`, you can also read a collection of free technical articles, sign up for a range of free newsletters, and receive exclusive discounts and offers on Packt books and eBooks.

Contributors

About the author

Chiheb Chebbi is an InfoSec enthusiast who has experience in various aspects of information security, focusing on the investigation of advanced cyber attacks and researching cyber espionage and APT attacks. Chiheb is currently pursuing an engineering degree in computer science at TEK-UP university in Tunisia.

His core interests are infrastructure penetration testing, deep learning, and malware analysis. In 2016, he was included in the Alibaba Security Research Center Hall Of Fame. His talk proposals were accepted by DeepSec 2017, Blackhat Europe 2016, and many world-class information security conferences.

I would like to thank my parents and friends who have always been a great support. I'd like to extend my thanks to Packt folks, especially Nithin, Heramb, and Komal for giving me the opportunity to get involved in this book.

About the reviewer

Aditya Mukherjee is a proficient information security professional, cybersecurity speaker, entrepreneur, cybercrime investigator, and columnist.

He has 10+ years of experience in different leadership roles across information security domains with various reputed organizations, specializing in the implementation of cybersecurity solutions, cyber transformation projects, and solving problems associated with security architecture, framework, and policies.

Packt is searching for authors like you

If you're interested in becoming an author for Packt, please visit authors.packtpub.com and apply today. We have worked with thousands of developers and tech professionals, just like you, to help them share their insight with the global tech community. You can make a general application, apply for a specific hot topic that we are recruiting an author for, or submit your own idea.

Table of Contents

Preface

Currently, machine learning techniques are some of the hottest trends in information technology. They impact on every aspect of our lives, and they affect every industry and field. Machine learning is a cyber weapon for information security professionals. In this book, you will not only explore the fundamentals of machine learning techniques, but will also learn the secrets to building a fully functional machine learning security system; we will not stop at building defensive layers. We will explore how to attack machine learning models with adversarial learning. *Mastering Machine Learning for Penetration Testing* will provide educational as well as practical value.

Who this book is for

Mastering Machine Learning for Penetration Testing is for pen testers and security professionals who are interested in learning techniques for breaking an intelligent security system. A basic knowledge of Python is needed, but no prior knowledge of machine learning is necessary.

What this book covers

Chapter 1, *Introduction to Machine Learning in Pentesting*, introduces reader to the fundamental concepts of the different machine learning models and algorithms, in addition to learning how to evaluate them. It then shows us how to prepare a machine learning development environment using many data science Python libraries.

Chapter 2, *Phishing Domain Detection*, guides us on how to build machine learning models to detect phishing emails and spam attempts using different algorithms and natural language processing (NLP).

Chapter 3, *Malware Detection with API Calls and PE Headers*, explains the different approaches to analyzing malware and malicious software, and later introduces us to some different techniques for building a machine learning-based malware detector.

Chapter 4, *Malware Detection with Deep Learning*, extends what we learned in the previous chapter to explore how to build artificial neural networks and deep learning to detect malware.

Chapter 5, *Botnet Detection with Machine Learning*, demonstrates how to build a botnet detector using the previously discussed techniques and publicly available botnet traffic datasets.

Chapter 6, *Machine Learning in Anomaly Detection Systems*, introduces us to the most important terminologies in anomaly detection and guides us to build machine learning anomaly detection systems.

Chapter 7, *Detecting Advanced Persistent Threats*, shows us how to build a fully working real-world threat hunting platform using the ELK stack, which is already loaded by machine learning capabilities.

Chapter 8, *Evading Intrusion Detection Systems with Adversarial Machine Learning*, demonstrates how to bypass machine learning systems using adversarial learning and studies some real-world cases, including bypassing next-generation intrusion detection systems.

Chapter 9, *Bypass Machine Learning Malware Detectors*, teaches us how to bypass machine learning-based malware detectors with adversarial learning and generative adversarial networks.

Chapter 10, *Best Practices for Machine Learning and Feature Engineering*, explores different feature engineering techniques, in addition to introducing readers to machine learning best practices to build reliable systems.

To get the most out of this book

We assume that the readers of this book are familiar with basic information security concepts and Python programming. Some of the demonstrations in this book require more practice and online research to delve into the concepts discussed.

Always check the GitHub repository of this book to check for updated code if you encounter any bugs, typos, or errors.

Download the example code files

You can download the example code files for this book from your account at www.packtpub.com. If you purchased this book elsewhere, you can visit www.packtpub.com/support and register to have the files emailed directly to you.

You can download the code files by following these steps:

1. Log in or register at www.packtpub.com.
2. Select the **SUPPORT** tab.
3. Click on **Code Downloads & Errata**.
4. Enter the name of the book in the **Search** box and follow the onscreen instructions.

Once the file is downloaded, please make sure that you unzip or extract the folder using the latest version of:

- WinRAR/7-Zip for Windows
- Zipeg/iZip/UnRarX for Mac
- 7-Zip/PeaZip for Linux

The code bundle for the book is also hosted on GitHub at https://github.com/PacktPublishing/Mastering-Machine-Learning-for-Penetration-Testing. In case there's an update to the code, it will be updated on the existing GitHub repository.

We also have other code bundles from our rich catalog of books and videos available at https://github.com/PacktPublishing/. Check them out!

Download the color images

We also provide a PDF file that has color images of the screenshots/diagrams used in this book. You can download it from https://www.packtpub.com/sites/default/files/downloads/MasteringMachineLearningforPenetrationTesting_ColorImages.pdf.

Conventions used

There are a number of text conventions used throughout this book.

CodeInText: Indicates code words in text, database table names, folder names, filenames, file extensions, pathnames, dummy URLs, user input, and Twitter handles. Here is an example: "First, check your Python version with the python --version command."

A block of code is set as follows:

```
from keras import [what_to_use]
from keras.models import Sequential
from keras.layers import Dense
```

When we wish to draw your attention to a particular part of a code block, the relevant lines or items are set in bold:

```
model = Sequential()
# N = number of neurons
# V = number of variable
model.add(Dense(N, input_dim=V, activation='relu'))
# S = number of neurons in the 2nd layer
model.add(Dense(S, activation='relu'))
model.add(Dense(1, activation='sigmoid')) # 1 output
```

Any command-line input or output is written as follows:

```
>>> import tensorflow as tf
>>> Message = tf.constant("Hello, world!")
>>> sess = tf.Session()
>>> print(sess.run(Message))
```

Bold: Indicates a new term, an important word, or words that you see onscreen.

Warnings or important notes appear like this.

Tips and tricks appear like this.

Get in touch

Feedback from our readers is always welcome.

General feedback: Email feedback@packtpub.com and mention the book title in the subject of your message. If you have questions about any aspect of this book, please email us at questions@packtpub.com.

Errata: Although we have taken every care to ensure the accuracy of our content, mistakes do happen. If you have found a mistake in this book, we would be grateful if you would report this to us. Please visit www.packtpub.com/submit-errata, selecting your book, clicking on the Errata Submission Form link, and entering the details.

Piracy: If you come across any illegal copies of our works in any form on the Internet, we would be grateful if you would provide us with the location address or website name. Please contact us at copyright@packtpub.com with a link to the material.

If you are interested in becoming an author: If there is a topic that you have expertise in and you are interested in either writing or contributing to a book, please visit authors.packtpub.com.

Reviews

Please leave a review. Once you have read and used this book, why not leave a review on the site that you purchased it from? Potential readers can then see and use your unbiased opinion to make purchase decisions, we at Packt can understand what you think about our products, and our authors can see your feedback on their book. Thank you!

For more information about Packt, please visit packtpub.com.

1
Introduction to Machine Learning in Pentesting

Currently, machine learning techniques are some of the hottest trends in information technology. They impact every aspect of our lives, and they affect every industry and field. Machine learning is a cyber weapon for information security professionals. In this book, readers will not only explore the fundamentals behind machine learning techniques, but will also learn the secrets to building a fully functional machine learning security system. We will not stop at building defensive layers; we will illustrate how to build offensive tools to attack and bypass security defenses. By the end of this book, you will be able to bypass machine learning security systems and use the models constructed in penetration testing (pentesting) missions.

In this chapter, we will cover:

- Machine learning models and algorithms
- Performance evaluation metrics
- Dimensionality reduction
- Ensemble learning
- Machine learning development environments and Python libraries
- Machine learning in penetration testing – promises and challenges

Technical requirements

In this chapter, we are going to build a development environment. Therefore, we are going to install the following Python machine learning libraries:

- NumPy
- SciPy

- TensorFlow
- Keras
- pandas
- MatplotLib
- scikit-learn
- NLTK
- Theano

You will also find all of the scripts and installation guides used in this GitHub repository: `https://github.com/PacktPublishing/Mastering-Machine-Learning-for-Penetration-Testing/tree/master/Chapter01`.

Artificial intelligence and machine learning

Making a machine think like a human is one of the oldest dreams. Machine learning techniques are used to help make predictions based on experiences and data.

Machine learning models and algorithms

In order to teach machines how to solve a large number of problems by themselves, we need to consider the different machine learning models. As you know, we need to feed the model with data; that is why machine learning models are divided, based on datasets entered (input), into four major categories: supervised learning, semi-supervised learning, unsupervised learning, and reinforcement. In this section, we are going to describe each model in a detailed way, in addition to exploring the most well-known algorithms used in every machine learning model. Before building machine learning systems, we need to know how things work underneath the surface.

Supervised

We talk about supervised machine learning when we have both the input variables and the output variables. In this case, we need to map the function (or pattern) between the two parties. The following are some of the most often used supervised machine learning algorithms.

Bayesian classifiers

According to the *Cambridge English Dictionary*, bias is the action of supporting or opposing a particular person or thing in an unfair way, allowing personal opinions to influence your judgment. Bayesian machine learning refers to having a prior belief, and updating it later by using data. Mathematically, it is based on the Bayes formula:

$$P(c|x) = \frac{P(x|c) \times P(c)}{P(x)}$$

One of the simplest Bayesian problems is randomly tossing a coin and trying to predict whether the output will be heads or tails. That is why we can identify Bayesian methodology as being probabilistic. Naive Bayes is very useful when you are using a small amount of data.

Support vector machines

A **support vector machine** (**SVM**) is a supervised machine learning model that works by identifying a hyperplane between represented data. The data can be represented in a multidimensional space. Thus, SVMs are widely used in classification models. In an SVM, the hyperplane that best separates the different classes will be used. In some cases, when we have different hyperplanes that separate different classes, identification of the correct one will be performed thanks to something called a **margin**, or a **gap**. The margin is the nearest distance between the hyperplanes and the data positions. You can take a look at the following representation to check for the margin:

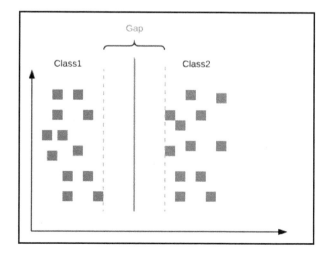

The hyperplane with the highest gap will be selected. If we choose the hyperplane with the shortest margin, we might face misclassification problems later. Don't be distracted by the previous graph; the hyperplane will not always be linear. Consider a case like the following:

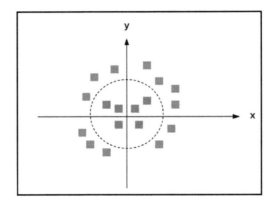

In the preceding situation, we can add a new axis, called the z axis, and apply a transformation using a kernel trick called a kernel function, where z=x^2+y^2. If you apply the transformation, the new graph will be as follows:

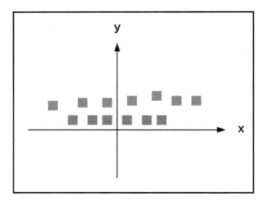

Now, we can identify the right hyperplane. The transformation is called a **kernel**. In the real world, finding a hyperplane is very hard. Thus, two important parameters, called regularization and gamma, play a huge role in the determination of the right hyperplane, and in every SVM classifier to obtain better accuracy in nonlinear hyperplane situations.

Decision trees

Decision trees are supervised learning algorithms used in decision making by representing data as trees upside-down with their roots at the top. The following is a graphical representation of a decision tree:

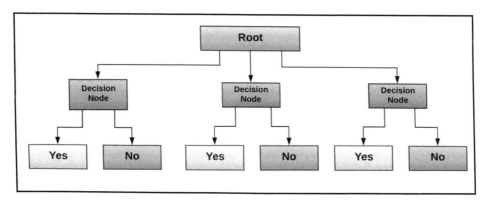

Data is represented thanks to the Iterative Dichotomiser 3 algorithm. Decision trees used in classification and regression problems are called CARTs. They were introduced by Leo Breiman.

Semi-supervised

Semi-supervised learning is an area between the two previously discussed models. In other words, if you are in a situation where you are using a small amount of labeled data in addition to unlabeled data, then you are performing semi-supervised learning. Semi-supervised learning is widely used in real-world applications, such as speech analysis, protein sequence classification, and web content classification. There are many semi-supervised methods, including generative models, low-density separation, and graph-based methods (discrete Markov Random Fields, manifold regularization, and mincut).

Unsupervised

In unsupervised learning, we don't have clear information about the output of the models. The following are some well-known unsupervised machine learning algorithms.

Artificial neural networks

Artificial networks are some of the hottest applications in artificial intelligence, especially machine learning. The main aim of artificial neural networks is building models that can learn like a human mind; in other words, we try to mimic the human mind. That is why, in order to learn how to build neural network systems, we need to have a clear understanding of how a human mind actually works. The human mind is an amazing entity. The mind is composed and wired by neurons. Neurons are responsible for transferring and processing information.

We all know that the human mind can perform a lot of tasks, like hearing, seeing, tasting, and many other complicated tasks. So logically, one might think that the mind is composed of many different areas, with each area responsible for a specific task, thanks to a specific algorithm. But this is totally wrong. According to research, all of the different parts of the human mind function thanks to one algorithm, not different algorithms. This hypothesis is called **the one algorithm hypothesis**.

Now we know that the mind works by using one algorithm. But what is this algorithm? How is it used? How is information processed with it?

To answer the preceding questions, we need to look at the logical representation of a neuron. The artificial representation of a human neuron is called a **perceptron**. A perceptron is represented by the following graph:

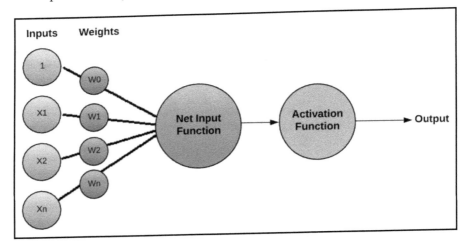

There are many **Activation Functions** used. You can view them as logical gates:

- **Step function**: A predefined threshold value.
- **Sigmoid function**:

$$f(x) = \frac{1}{1 + e^{-x}}$$

- **Tanh function**:

$$f(x) = \frac{2}{1 + e^{-2x}} - 1$$

- **ReLu function**:

$$f(x) = \begin{cases} 0 \, for \, x < 0 \\ x \, for \, x >= 0 \end{cases}$$

Many fully connected perceptrons comprise what we call a **Multi-Layer Perceptron (MLP)** network. A typical neural network contains the following:

- An input layer
- Hidden layers
- Output layers

We will discuss the term **deep learning** once we have more than three hidden layers. There are many types of deep learning networks used in the world:

- **Convolutional neural networks (CNNs)**
- **Recursive neural networks (RNNs)**
- **Long short-term memory (LSTM)**
- Shallow neural networks
- **Autoencoders (AEs)**
- Restricted Boltzmann machines

Don't worry; we will discuss the preceding algorithms in detail in future chapters.

To build deep learning models, we follow five steps, suggested by Dr. Jason Brownlee. The five steps are as follows:

1. Network definition
2. Network compiling
3. Network fitting
4. Network evaluation
5. Prediction

Linear regression

Linear regression is a statistical and machine learning technique. It is widely used to understand the relationship between inputs and outputs. We use linear regression when we have numerical values.

Logistic regression

Logistic regression is also a statistical and machine learning technique, used as a binary classifier - in other words, when the outputs are classes (yes/no, true/false, 0/1, and so on).

Clustering with k-means

k-Nearest Neighbors (kNN) is a well-known clustering method. It is based on finding similarities in data points, or what we call the feature similarity. Thus, this algorithm is simple, and is widely used to solve many classification problems, like recommendation systems, anomaly detection, credit ratings, and so on. However, it requires a high amount of memory. While it is a supervised learning model, it should be fed by labeled data, and the outputs are known. We only need to map the function that relates the two parties. A kNN algorithm is non-parametric. Data is represented as feature vectors. You can see it as a mathematical representation:

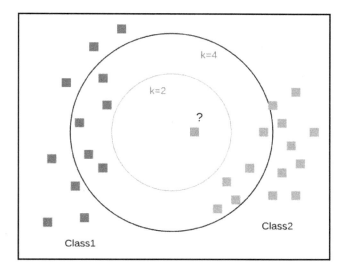

The classification is done like a vote; to know the class of the data selected, you must first compute the distance between the selected item and the other, training item. But how can we calculate these distances?

Generally, we have two major methods for calculating. We can use the Euclidean distance:

$$E(x, y) = \sqrt{\sum_{i=0}^{n}(x_i - y_i)^2}$$

Or, we can use the cosine similarity:

$$Similarity = \cos(\varnothing) = \frac{A.B}{\|A\| \times \|B\|}$$

The second step is choosing k the nearest distances (k can be picked arbitrarily). Finally, we conduct a vote, based on a confidence level. In other words, the data will be assigned to the class with the largest probability.

Reinforcement

In the reinforcement machine learning model, the agent is in interaction with its environment, so it learns from experience, by collecting data during the process; the goal is optimizing what we call a long term **reward**. You can view it as a game with a scoring system. The following graph illustrates a reinforcement model:

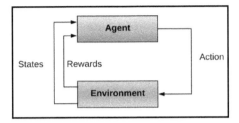

Performance evaluation

Evaluation is a key step in every methodological operation. After building a product or a system, especially a machine learning model, we need to have a clear vision about its performance, to make sure that it will act as intended later on. In order to evaluate a machine learning performance, we need to use well-defined parameters and insights. To compute the different evaluation metrics, we need to use four important parameters:

- True positive
- False positive
- True negative
- False negative

The notations for the preceding parameters are as follows:

- *tp*: True positive
- *fp*: False positive
- *tn*: True negative
- *fn*: False negative

There are many machine learning evaluation metrics, such as the following:

- **Precision**: Precision, or positive predictive value, is the ratio of positive samples that are correctly classified divided by the total number of positive classified samples:

$$precision = \frac{tp}{tp + fp}$$

- **Recall**: Recall, or the true positive rate, is the ratio of true positive classifications divided by the total number of positive samples in the dataset:

$$Recall = \frac{tp}{tp + fn}$$

- **F-Score**: The F-score, or F-measure, is a measure that combines the precision and recall in one harmonic formula:

$$F - Score = 2 \times \frac{Precision \times Recall}{Precision + Recall}$$

- **Accuracy**: Accuracy is the ratio of the total correctly classified samples divided by the total number of samples. This measure is not sufficient by itself, because it is used when we have an equal number of classes.

- **Confusion matrix**: The confusion matrix is a graphical representation of the performance of a given machine learning model. It summarizes the performance of each class in a classification problem.

Dimensionality reduction

Dimensionality reduction is used to reduce the dimensionality of a dataset. It is really helpful in cases where the problem becomes intractable, when the number of variables increases. By using the term dimensionality, we are referring to the features. One of the basic reduction techniques is feature engineering.

Generally, we have many dimensionality reduction algorithms:

- **Low variance filter**: Dropping variables that have low variance, compared to others.
- **High correlation filter**: This identifies the variables with high correlation, by using pearson or polychoric, and selects one of them using the **Variance Inflation Factor (VIF)**.
- **Backward feature elimination**: This is done by computing the **sum of square of error (SSE)** after eliminating each variable n times.
- **Linear Discriminant Analysis (LDA)**: This reduces the number of dimensions, n, from the original to the number of classes—1 number of features.
- **Principal Component Analysis (PCA)**: This is a statistical procedure that transforms variables into a new set of variables (principle components).

Improving classification with ensemble learning

In many cases, when you build a machine learning model, you receive low accuracy and low results. In order to get good results, we can use ensemble learning techniques. This can be done by combining many machine learning techniques into one predictive model.

We can categorize ensemble learning techniques into two categories:

- **Parallel ensemble methods**—The following graph illustrates how parallel ensemble learning works:

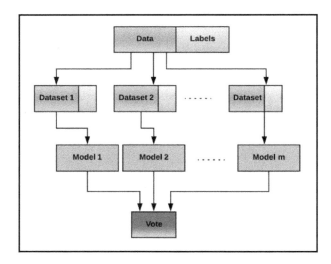

- **Sequential ensemble methods**—The following graph illustrates how sequential ensemble learning works:

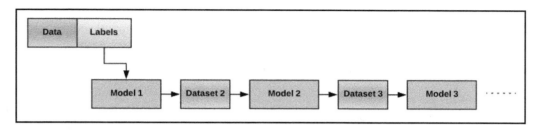

The following are the three most used ensemble learning techniques:

- **Bootstrap aggregating** (**bagging**): This involves building separate models and combining them by using model averaging techniques, like weighted average and majority vote.
- **Boosting**: This is a sequential ensemble learning technique. Gradient boosting is one of the most used boosting techniques.
- **Stacking**: This is like boosting, but it uses a new model to combine submodels.

Machine learning development environments and Python libraries

At this point, we have acquired knowledge about the fundamentals behind the most used machine learning algorithms. Starting with this section, we will go deeper, walking through a hands-on learning experience to build machine learning-based security projects. We are not going to stop there; throughout the next chapters, we will learn how malicious attackers can bypass intelligent security systems. Now, let's put what we have learned so far into practice. If you are reading this book, you probably have some experience with Python. Good for you, because you have a foundation for learning how to build machine learning security systems.

I bet you are wondering, why Python? This is a great question. According to the latest research, Python is one of the most, if not *the* most, used programming languages in data science, especially machine learning. The most well-known machine learning libraries are for Python. Let's discover the Python libraries and utilities required to build a machine learning model.

NumPy

The numerical Python library is one of the most used libraries in mathematics and logical operations on arrays. It is loaded with many linear algebra functionalities, which are very useful in machine learning. And, of course, it is open source, and is supported by many operating systems.

To install NumPy, use the `pip` utility by typing the following command:

```
#pip install numpy
```

Now, you can start using it by importing it. The following script is a simple array printing example:

In addition, you can use a lot of mathematical functions, like `cosine`, `sine`, and so on.

SciPy

Scientific Python (SciPy) is like NumPy—an amazing Python package, loaded with a large number of scientific functions and utilities. For more details, you can visit `https://www.scipy.org/getting-started.html`:

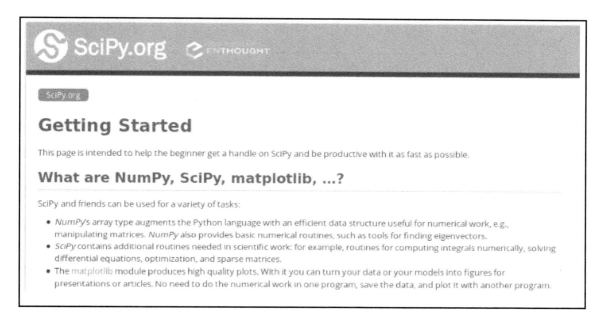

TensorFlow

If you have been into machine learning for a while, you will have heard of TensorFlow, or have even used it to build a machine learning model or to feed artificial neural networks. It is an amazing open source project, developed essentially and supported by Google:

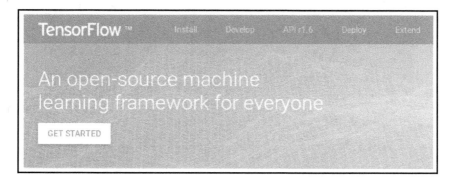

The following is the main architecture of TensorFlow, according to the official website:

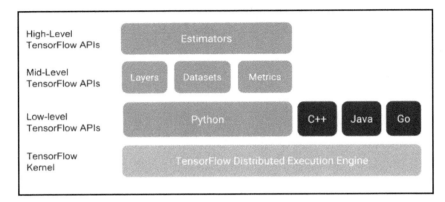

If it is your first time using TensorFlow, it is highly recommended to visit the project's official website at https://www.tensorflow.org/get_started/. Let's install it on our machine, and discover some of its functionalities. There are many possibilities for installing it; you can use native PIP, Docker, Anaconda, or Virtualenv.

Let's suppose that we are going to install it on an Ubuntu machine (it also supports the other operating systems). First, check your Python version with the `python --version` command:

Install PIP and Virtualenv using the following command:

```
sudo apt-get install python-pip python-dev python-virtualenv
```

```
azureuser@tensorflow: ~                                            —    □    ×

azureuser@tensorflow:~$  sudo apt-get install python-pip python-dev python-virtualenv
Reading package lists... Done
Building dependency tree
Reading state information... Done
The following additional packages will be installed:
  build-essential cpp cpp-5 dpkg-dev fakeroot g++ g++-5 gcc gcc-5 libalgorithm-diff-perl
  libalgorithm-diff-xs-perl libalgorithm-merge-perl libasan2 libatomic1 libc-dev-bin libc6-dev
  libcc1-0 libcilkrts5 libdpkg-perl libexpat1-dev libfakeroot libfile-fcntllock-perl
  libgcc-5-dev libgomp1 libisl15 libitm1 liblsan0 libmpc3 libmpx0 libpython-all-dev
  libpython-dev libpython2.7-dev libquadmath0 libstdc++-5-dev libtsan0 libubsan0 linux-libc-dev
  make manpages-dev python-all python-all-dev python-pip-whl python-pkg-resources
  python-setuptools python-wheel python2.7-dev python3-virtualenv virtualenv
Suggested packages:
  cpp-doc gcc-5-locales debian-keyring g++-multilib g++-5-multilib gcc-5-doc libstdc++6-5-dbg
  gcc-multilib autoconf automake libtool flex bison gdb gcc-doc gcc-5-multilib libgcc1-dbg
  libgomp1-dbg libitm1-dbg libatomic1-dbg libasan2-dbg liblsan0-dbg libtsan0-dbg libubsan0-dbg
  libcilkrts5-dbg libmpx0-dbg libquadmath0-dbg glibc-doc libstdc++-5-doc make-doc
  python-setuptools-doc
The following NEW packages will be installed:
  build-essential cpp cpp-5 dpkg-dev fakeroot g++ g++-5 gcc gcc-5 libalgorithm-diff-perl
  libalgorithm-diff-xs-perl libalgorithm-merge-perl libasan2 libatomic1 libc-dev-bin libc6-dev
  libcc1-0 libcilkrts5 libdpkg-perl libexpat1-dev libfakeroot libfile-fcntllock-perl
  libgcc-5-dev libgomp1 libisl15 libitm1 liblsan0 libmpc3 libmpx0 libpython-all-dev
  libpython-dev libpython2.7-dev libquadmath0 libstdc++-5-dev libtsan0 libubsan0 linux-libc-dev
  make manpages-dev python-all python-all-dev python-dev python-pip python-pip-whl
  python-pkg-resources python-setuptools python-virtualenv python-wheel python2.7-dev
  python3-virtualenv virtualenv
0 upgraded, 51 newly installed, 0 to remove and 1 not upgraded.
```

Now, the packages are installed:

```
azureuser@tensorflow: ~                                            —    □    ×

Setting up fakeroot (1.20.2-1ubuntu1) ...
update-alternatives: using /usr/bin/fakeroot-sysv to provide /usr/bin/fakeroot (fakeroot) in auto
mode
Setting up libalgorithm-diff-perl (1.19.03-1) ...
Setting up libalgorithm-diff-xs-perl (0.04-4build1) ...
Setting up libalgorithm-merge-perl (0.08-3) ...
Setting up libexpat1-dev:amd64 (2.1.0-7ubuntu0.16.04.3) ...
Setting up libfile-fcntllock-perl (0.22-3) ...
Setting up libpython2.7-dev:amd64 (2.7.12-1ubuntu0~16.04.3) ...
Setting up libpython-dev:amd64 (2.7.12-1~16.04) ...
Setting up libpython-all-dev:amd64 (2.7.12-1~16.04) ...
Setting up manpages-dev (4.04-2) ...
Setting up python-all (2.7.12-1~16.04) ...
Setting up python2.7-dev (2.7.12-1ubuntu0~16.04.3) ...
Setting up python-dev (2.7.12-1~16.04) ...
Setting up python-all-dev (2.7.12-1~16.04) ...
Setting up python-pip-whl (8.1.1-2ubuntu0.4) ...
Setting up python-pip (8.1.1-2ubuntu0.4) ...
Setting up python-pkg-resources (20.7.0-1) ...
Setting up python-setuptools (20.7.0-1) ...
Setting up python-virtualenv (15.0.1+ds-3ubuntu1) ...
Setting up python-wheel (0.29.0-1) ...
Setting up python3-virtualenv (15.0.1+ds-3ubuntu1) ...
Setting up virtualenv (15.0.1+ds-3ubuntu1) ...
Processing triggers for libc-bin (2.23-0ubuntu10) ...
azureuser@tensorflow:~$
```

Create a new repository using the `mkdir` command:

```
#mkdir TF-project
```

Create a new Virtualenv by typing the following command:

```
virtualenv --system-site-packages TF-project
```

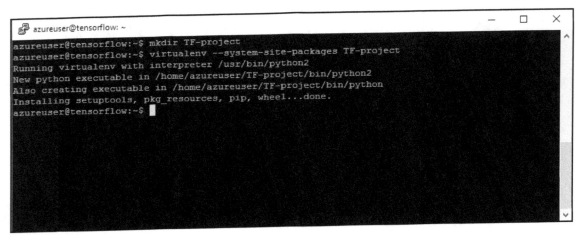

Then, type the following command:

```
source   <Directory_Here>/bin/activate
```

Upgrade TensorFlow by using the `pip install -upgrade tensorflow` command:

```
azureuser@tensorflow: ~/TF-project                                        —  □  ×
azureuser@tensorflow:~/TF-project$ source /home/azureuser/TF-project/bin/activate
(TF-project) azureuser@tensorflow:~/TF-project$ pip install --upgrade tensorflow
Collecting tensorflow
  Downloading tensorflow-1.6.0-cp27-cp27mu-manylinux1_x86_64.whl (45.9MB)
    100% |                                      | 45.9MB 29kB/s
Collecting astor>=0.6.0 (from tensorflow)
  Downloading astor-0.6.2-py2.py3-none-any.whl
Collecting protobuf>=3.4.0 (from tensorflow)
  Downloading protobuf-3.5.2.post1-cp27-cp27mu-manylinux1_x86_64.whl (6.4MB)
    100% |                                      | 6.4MB 195kB/s
Collecting gast>=0.2.0 (from tensorflow)
  Downloading gast-0.2.0.tar.gz
Collecting tensorboard<1.7.0,>=1.6.0 (from tensorflow)
  Downloading tensorboard-1.6.0-py2-none-any.whl (3.0MB)
    100% |                                      | 3.1MB 445kB/s
Collecting six>=1.10.0 (from tensorflow)
  Downloading six-1.11.0-py2.py3-none-any.whl
```

```
>>> import tensorflow as tf
>>> Message = tf.constant("Hello, world!")
>>> sess = tf.Session()
>>> print(sess.run(Message))
```

The following are the full steps to display a `Hello World!` message:

```
azureuser@tensorflow: ~/TF-project                                    —    □    ✕

(TF-project) azureuser@tensorflow:~/TF-project$ python
Python 2.7.12 (default, Dec  4 2017, 14:50:18)
[GCC 5.4.0 20160609] on linux2
Type "help", "copyright", "credits" or "license" for more information.
>>> import tensorflow as tf
>>> Message = tf.constant("Hello World!")
>>> sess = tf.Session()
2018-03-19 21:10:10.062507: I tensorflow/core/platform/cpu_feature_guard.cc:140] Your CPU
t this TensorFlow binary was not compiled to use: AVX2 FMA
>>> print(sess.run(Message))
Hello World!
>>>
```

Keras

Keras is a widely used Python library for building deep learning models. It is so easy, because it is built on top of TensorFlow. The best way to build deep learning models is to follow the previously discussed steps:

1. Loading data
2. Defining the model
3. Compiling the model
4. Fitting
5. Evaluation
6. Prediction

Before building the models, please ensure that SciPy and NumPy are preconfigured. To check, open the Python command-line interface and type, for example, the following command, to check the NumPy version:

```
>>>print numpy.__version__
```

To install Keras, just use the PIP utility:

```
$ pip install keras
```

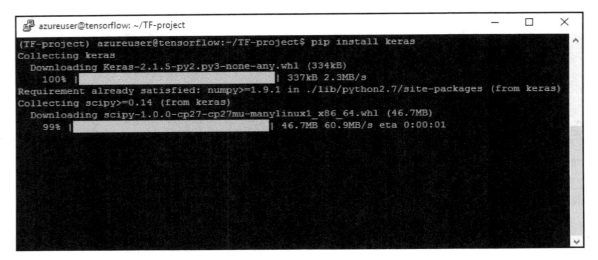

And of course to check the version, type the following command:

```
>>> print keras.__version__
```

To import from Keras, use the following:

```
from keras import [what_to_use]
from keras.models import Sequential
from keras.layers import Dense
```

Now, we need to load data:

```
dataset = numpy.loadtxt("DATASET_HERE", delimiter=",")
I = dataset[:,0:8]
O = dataset[:,8]
#the data is splitted into Inputs (I) and Outputs (O)
```

You can use any publicly available dataset. Next, we need to create the model:

```
model = Sequential()
# N = number of neurons
# V = number of variable
model.add(Dense(N, input_dim=V, activation='relu'))
# S = number of neurons in the 2nd layer
model.add(Dense(S, activation='relu'))
model.add(Dense(1, activation='sigmoid')) # 1 output
```

Now, we need to compile the model:

```
model.compile(loss='binary_crossentropy', optimizer='adam',
metrics=['accuracy'])
```

And we need to fit the model:

```
model.fit(I, O, epochs=E, batch_size=B)
```

As discussed previously, evaluation is a key step in machine learning; so, to evaluate our model, we use:

```
scores = model.evaluate(I, O)
print("\n%s: %.2f%%" % (model.metrics_names[1], scores[1]*100))
```

To make a prediction, add the following line:

```
predictions = model.predict(Some_Input_Here)
```

pandas

pandas is an open source Python library, known for its high performance; it was developed by Wes McKinney. It quickly manipulates data. That is why it is widely used in many fields in academia and commercial activities. Like the previous packages, it is supported by many operating systems.

To install it on an Ubuntu machine, type the following command:

```
sudo apt-get install python-pandas
```

Basically, it manipulates three major data structures - data frames, series, and panels:

```
>> import pandas as pd
>>>import numpy as np
 data = np.array(['p','a','c','k','t'])
 SR = pd.Series(data)
 print SR
```

I resumed all of the previous lines in this screenshot:

Matplotlib

As you know, visualization plays a huge role in gaining insights from data, and is also very important in machine learning. Matplotlib is a visualization library used for plotting by data scientists. You can get a clearer understanding by visiting its official website at `https://matplotlib.org`:

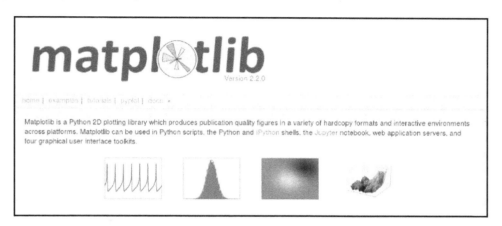

To install it on an Ubuntu machine, use the following command:

```
sudo apt-get install python3-matplotlib
```

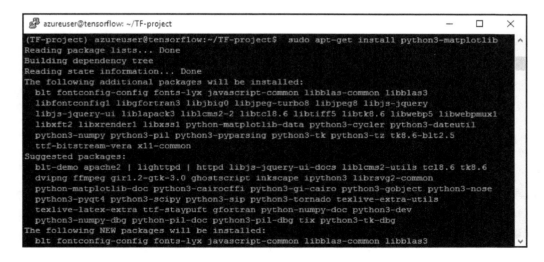

To import the required packages, use `import`:

```
import matplotlib.pyplot as plt
import numpy as np
```

Use this example to prepare the data:

```
x = np.linspace(0, 20, 50)
```

To plot it, add this line:

```
plt.plot(x, x, label='linear')
```

To add a legend, use the following:

```
plt.legend()
```

Now, let's show the plot:

```
plt.show()
```

Voila! This is our plot:

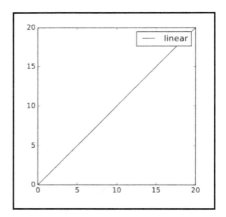

scikit-learn

I highly recommend this amazing Python library. scikit-learn is fully loaded, with various capabilities, including machine learning features. The official website of scikit-learn is `http://scikit-learn.org/`. To download it, use PIP, as previously discussed:

```
pip install -U scikit-learn
```

```
azureuser@tensorflow: ~/TF-project                                    —    □    ×
(TF-project) azureuser@tensorflow:~/TF-project$ pip install -U scikit-learn
Collecting scikit-learn
  Downloading scikit_learn-0.19.1-cp27-cp27mu-manylinux1_x86_64.whl (12.2MB)
    100% |████████████████████████████████| 12.2MB 97kB/s
Installing collected packages: scikit-learn
Successfully installed scikit-learn-0.19.1
(TF-project) azureuser@tensorflow:~/TF-project$ █
```

NLTK

Natural language processing is one of the most used applications in machine learning projects. NLTK is a Python package that helps developers and data scientists manage and manipulate large quantities of text. NLTK can be installed by using the following command:

```
pip install -U nltk
```

```
azureuser@tensorflow: ~/TF-project                                    —    □    ×
(TF-project) azureuser@tensorflow:~/TF-project$ pip install -U nltk
Collecting nltk
  Downloading nltk-3.2.5.tar.gz (1.2MB)
    100% |████████████████████████████████| 1.2MB 962kB/s
Requirement already up-to-date: six in ./lib/python2.7/site-packages (from nltk)
Building wheels for collected packages: nltk
  Running setup.py bdist_wheel for nltk ... done
  Stored in directory: /home/azureuser/.cache/pip/wheels/18/9c/1f/276bc3f421614062468cb1c9d
695e6086d0c73d67ea363c501
Successfully built nltk
Installing collected packages: nltk
Successfully installed nltk-3.2.5
(TF-project) azureuser@tensorflow:~/TF-project$ █
```

Now, import nltk:

```
>>> import nltk
```

Install `nltk` packages with:

```
> nltk.download()
```

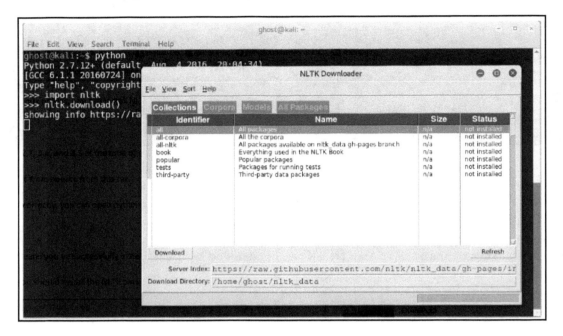

You can install all of the packages:

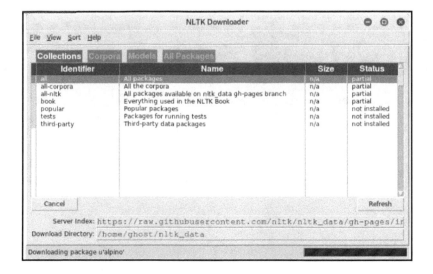

If you are using a command-line environment, you just need to follow the steps:

```
azureuser@tensorflow: ~/TF-project                                    —    □    ×

Download which package (l=list; x=cancel)?
  Identifier> 1
Packages:
  [ ] abc................. Australian Broadcasting Commission 2006
  [ ] alpino.............. Alpino Dutch Treebank
  [ ] averaged_perceptron_tagger Averaged Perceptron Tagger
  [ ] averaged_perceptron_tagger_ru Averaged Perceptron Tagger (Russian)
  [ ] basque_grammars..... Grammars for Basque
  [ ] biocreative_ppi..... BioCreAtIvE (Critical Assessment of Information
                           Extraction Systems in Biology)
  [ ] bllip_wsj_no_aux.... BLLIP Parser: WSJ Model
  [ ] book_grammars....... Grammars from NLTK Book
  [ ] brown............... Brown Corpus
  [ ] brown_tei........... Brown Corpus (TEI XML Version)
  [ ] cess_cat............ CESS-CAT Treebank
  [ ] cess_esp............ CESS-ESP Treebank
  [ ] chat80.............. Chat-80 Data Files
  [ ] city_database....... City Database
  [ ] cmudict............. The Carnegie Mellon Pronouncing Dictionary (0.6)
  [ ] comparative_sentences Comparative Sentence Dataset
  [ ] comtrans............ ComTrans Corpus Sample
  [ ] conll2000........... CONLL 2000 Chunking Corpus
  [ ] conll2002........... CONLL 2002 Named Entity Recognition Corpus
Hit Enter to continue:
```

If you hit `all`, you will download all of the packages:

```
azureuser@tensorflow: ~/TF-project                                    —    □    ×
   d) Download   l) List   u) Update   c) Config   h) Help   q) Quit
-----------------------------------------------------------------------
Downloader> d

Download which package (l=list; x=cancel)?
  Identifier> all
    Downloading collection u'all'
    |
    | Downloading package abc to /home/azureuser/nltk_data...
    |   Unzipping corpora/abc.zip.
    | Downloading package alpino to /home/azureuser/nltk_data...
    |   Unzipping corpora/alpino.zip.
    | Downloading package biocreative_ppi to
    |     /home/azureuser/nltk_data...
    |   Unzipping corpora/biocreative_ppi.zip.
    | Downloading package brown to /home/azureuser/nltk_data...
    |   Unzipping corpora/brown.zip.
    | Downloading package brown_tei to /home/azureuser/nltk_data...
    |   Unzipping corpora/brown_tei.zip.
    | Downloading package cess_cat to /home/azureuser/nltk_data...
    |   Unzipping corpora/cess_cat.zip.
    | Downloading package cess_esp to /home/azureuser/nltk_data...
    |   Unzipping corpora/cess_esp.zip.
    | Downloading package chat80 to /home/azureuser/nltk_data...
```

Theano

Optimization and speed are two key factors to building a machine learning model. Theano is a Python package that optimizes implementations and gives you the ability to take advantage of the GPU. To install it, use the following command:

```
pip install theano
```

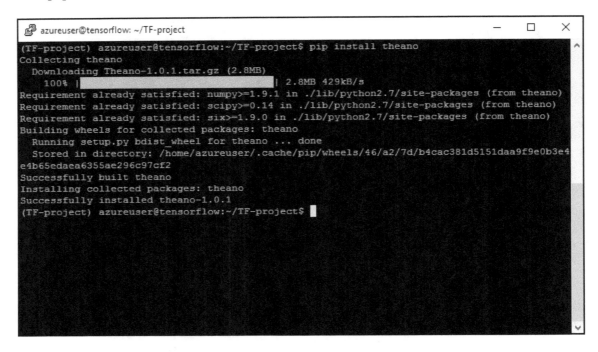

To import all Theano modules, type:

```
>>> from theano import *
```

Here, we imported a sub-package called `tensor`:

```
>>> import theano.tensor as T
```

Let's suppose that we want to add two numbers:

```
>>> from theano import function
>>> a = T.dscalar('a')
>>> b = T.dscalar('b')
>>> c = a + b
>>> f = function([a, b], c)
```

The following are the full steps:

```
azureuser@tensorflow: ~/TF-project                              —    □    ×
(TF-project) azureuser@tensorflow:~/TF-project$ python
Python 2.7.12 (default, Dec  4 2017, 14:50:18)
[GCC 5.4.0 20160609] on linux2
Type "help", "copyright", "credits" or "license" for more information.
>>> from theano import *
WARNING (theano.tensor.blas): Using NumPy C-API based implementation for BLAS functions.
>>> import theano.tensor as T
>>> from theano import function
>>> a= T.dscalar('a')
>>> b= T.dscalar('b')
>>> c= a+b
>>> f = function([a,b],c)
>>>
```

By now, we have acquired the fundamental skills to install and use the most common Python libraries used in machine learning projects. I assume that you have already installed all of the previous packages on your machine. In the subsequent chapters, we are going to use most of these packages to build fully working information security machine learning projects.

Machine learning in penetration testing - promises and challenges

Machine learning is now a necessary aspect of every modern project. Combining mathematics and cutting-edge optimization techniques and tools can provide amazing results. Applying machine learning and analytics to information security is a step forward in defending against advanced real-world attacks and threats.

Hackers are always trying to use new, sophisticated techniques to attack modern organizations. Thus, as security professionals, we need to keep ourselves updated and deploy the required safeguards to protect assets. Many researchers have shown thousands of proposals to build defensive systems based on machine learning techniques. For example, the following are some information security models:

- **Supervised learning**:
    - Network traffic profiling
    - Spam filtering
    - Malware detection

- **Semi-supervised learning**:
    - Network anomaly detection
    - C2 detection

- **Unsupervised learning**:
    - User behavior analytics
    - Insider threat detection
    - Malware family identification

As you can see, there are great applications to help protect the valuable assets of modern organizations. But generally, black hat hackers do not use classic techniques anymore. Nowadays, the use of machine learning techniques is shifting from defensive techniques to offensive systems. We are moving from a defensive to an offensive position. In fact, building defensive layers with artificial intelligence and machine learning alone is not enough; having an understanding of how to leverage those techniques to perform ferocious attacks is needed, and should be added to your technical skills when performing penetration testing missions. Adding offensive machine learning tools to your pentesting arsenal is very useful when it comes to simulating cutting-edge attacks. While a lot of these offensive applications are still for research purposes, we will try to build our own projects, to get a glimpse of how attackers are building offensive tools and cyber weapons to attack modern companies. Maybe you can use them later, in your penetration testing operations.

Deep Exploit

Many great publicly available tools appeared lately that use machine learning capabilities to leverage penetration testing to another level. One of these tools is Deep Exploit. It was presented at black hat conference 2018. It is a fully automated penetration test tool linked with metasploit. This great tool uses uses reinforcement learning (self-learning).

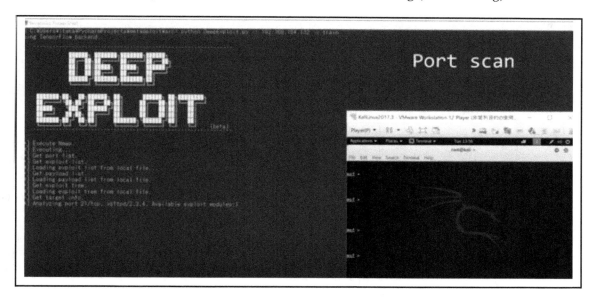

It is able to perform the following tasks:

- Intelligence gathering
- Threat modeling
- Vulnerability analysis
- Exploitation
- Post-exploitation
- Reporting

To download Deep Exploit visit its official GitHub repository: `https://github.com/13o-bbr-bbq/machine_learning_security/tree/master/DeepExploit`.

It is consists of a machine learning model (A3C) and metasploit. This is a high level overview of Deep Exploit architecture:

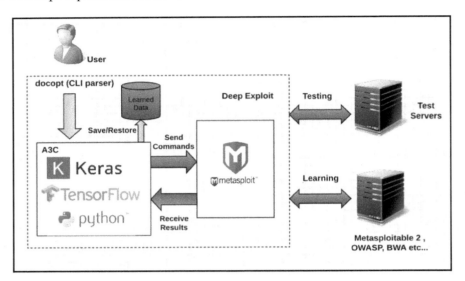

The required environment to make Deep Exploit works properly is the following:

- Kali Linux 2017.3 (guest OS on VMWare)
  - Memory: 8.0GB
  - Metasploit framework 4.16.15-dev
- Windows 10 Home 64-bit (Host OS)
  - CPU: Intel(R) Core(TM) i7-6500U 2.50GHz
  - Memory: 16.0GB
  - Python 3.6.1 (Anaconda3)
  - TensorFlow 1.4.0
  - Keras 2.1.2

Summary

Now we have learned the most commonly used machine learning techniques; before diving into practical labs, we need to acquire a fair understanding of how these models actually work. Our practical experience will start from the next chapter.

After reading this chapter, I assume that we can build our own development environment. The second chapter will show us what it takes to defend against advanced, computer-based, social engineering attacks, and we will learn how to build a smart phishing detector. Like in every chapter, we will start by learning the techniques behind the attacks, and we will walk through the practical steps in order to build a phishing detecting system.

Questions

1. Although machine learning is an interesting concept, there are limited business applications in which it is useful. (True | False)
2. Machine learning applications are too complex to run in the cloud. (True | False)
3. For two runs of k-means clustering, is it expected to get the same clustering results? (Yes | No)
4. Predictive models having target attributes with discrete values can be termed as:

    (a) Regression models
    (b) Classification models

5. Which of the following techniques perform operations similar to dropouts in a neural network?

    (a) Stacking
    (b) Bagging
    (c) Boosting

6. Which architecture of a neural network would be best suited for solving an image recognition problem?

    (a) Convolutional neural network
    (b) Recurrent neural network
    (c) Multi-Layer Perceptron
    (d) Perceptron

7. How does deep learning differ from conventional machine learning?

    (a) Deep learning algorithms can handle more data and run with less supervision from data scientists.
    (b) Machine learning is simpler, and requires less oversight by data analysts than deep learning does.

(c) There are no real differences between the two; they are the same tool, with different names.

8. Which of the following is a technique frequently used in machine learning projects?

(a) Classification of data into categories.
(b) Grouping similar objects into clusters.
(c) Identifying relationships between events to predict when one will follow the other.
(d) All of the above.

Further reading

To save you some effort, I have prepared a list of useful resources, to help you go deeper into exploring the techniques we have discussed.

Recommended books:

- *Python Machine Learning - Second Edition* by Sebastian Raschka and Vahid Mirjalili: https://www.packtpub.com/big-data-and-business-intelligence/python-machine-learning-second-edition
- *Building Machine Learning Systems with Python* by Luis Pedro Coelho and Willi Richert: https://www.amazon.com/Building-Machine-Learning-Systems-Python/dp/1782161406
- *Data Science from Scratch: First Principles with Python* by Joel Grus: https://www.amazon.com/Data-Science-Scratch-Principles-Python/dp/149190142X/ref=pd_sim_14_4?_encoding=UTF8&pd_rd_i=149190142X&pd_rd_r=506TTMZ93CK4Q4KZWDRM&pd_rd_w=5Eqf8&pd_rd_wg=1HMzv&psc=1&refRID=506TTMZ93CK4Q4KZWDRM

Recommended websites and online courses:

- **Machine Learning Mastery:** https://machinelearningmastery.com
- **Coursera—Machine Learning (Andrew Ng):** https://www.coursera.org/learn/machine-learning#syllabus
- **Neural Networks for Machine Learning:** https://www.coursera.org/learn/neural-networks

Phishing Domain Detection 2

Social engineering is one of the most dangerous threats facing every individual and modern organization. Phishing is a well-known, computer-based, social engineering technique. Attackers use disguised email addresses as a weapon to target large companies. With the huge number of phishing emails received every day, companies are not able to detect all of them. That is why new techniques and safeguards are needed to defend against phishing. This chapter will present the steps required to build three different machine learning-based projects to detect phishing attempts, using cutting-edge Python machine learning libraries.

In this chapter, we will cover:

- A social engineering overview
- The steps for social engineering penetration testing
- Building a real-time phishing attack detector using different machine learning models:
    - Phishing detection with logistic regression
    - Phishing detection with decision trees
    - Spam email detection with **natural language processing** (**NLP**)

Technical requirements

In this chapter, we are going to use the following Python libraries:

- scikit-learn Python (≥ 2.7 or ≥ 3.3)
- NumPy (≥ 1.8.2)
- NLTK

If you have not installed them yet, please make sure that they are installed before moving forward with this chapter. You can find the code files at `https://github.com/PacktPublishing/Mastering-Machine-Learning-for-Penetration-Testing/tree/master/Chapter02`.

Social engineering overview

Social engineering, by definition, is the psychological manipulation of a person to get useful and sensitive information from them, which can later be used to compromise a system. In other words, criminals use social engineering to gain confidential information from people, by taking advantage of human behavior.

Social Engineering Engagement Framework

The **Social Engineering Engagement Framework** (**SEEF**) is a framework developed by Dominique C. Brack and Alexander Bahmram. It summarizes years of experience in information security and defending against social engineering. The stakeholders of the framework are organizations, governments, and individuals (personals). Social engineering engagement management goes through three steps:

1. **Pre-engagement process**: Preparing the social engineering operation
2. **During-engagement process**: The engagement occurs
3. **Post-engagement process**: Delivering a report

There are many social engineering techniques used by criminals:

- **Baiting**: Convincing the victim to reveal information, promising him a reward or a gift.
- **Impersonation**: Pretending to be someone else.
- **Dumpster diving**: Collecting valuable information (papers with addresses, emails, and so on) from dumpsters.
- **Shoulder surfing**: Spying on other peoples' machines from behind them, while they are typing.
- **Phishing**: This is the most often used technique; it occurs when an attacker, masquerading as a trusted entity, dupes a victim into opening an email, instant message, or text message.

Steps of social engineering penetration testing

Penetration testing simulates a black hat hacker attack in order to evaluate the security posture of a company for deploying the required safeguard. Penetration testing is a methodological process, and it goes through well-defined steps. There are many types of penetration testing:

- White box pentesting
- Black box pentesting
- Grey box pentesting

To perform a social engineering penetration test, you need to follow the following steps:

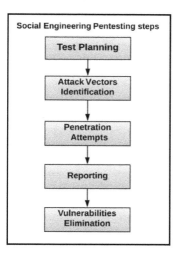

Building real-time phishing attack detectors using different machine learning models

In the next sections, we are going to learn how to build machine learning phishing detectors. We will cover the following two methods:

- Phishing detection with logistic regression
- Phishing detection with decision trees

Phishing detection with logistic regression

In this section, we are going to build a phishing detector from scratch with a logistic regression algorithm. Logistic regression is a well-known statistical technique used to make binomial predictions (two classes).

Like in every machine learning project, we will need data to feed our machine learning model. For our model, we are going to use the UCI Machine Learning Repository (Phishing Websites Data Set). You can check it out at `https://archive.ics.uci.edu/ml/datasets/Phishing+Websites`:

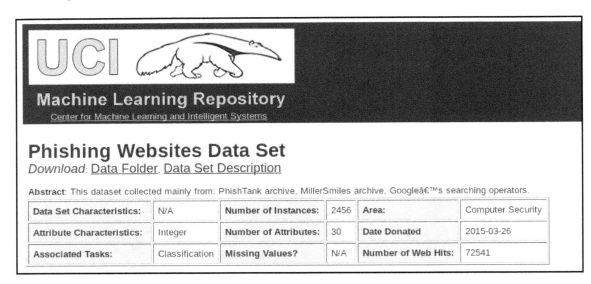

Phishing Websites Data Set
Download: Data Folder. Data Set Description

Abstract: This dataset collected mainly from: PhishTank archive, MillerSmiles archive, Google's searching operators.

Data Set Characteristics:	N/A	Number of Instances:	2456	Area:	Computer Security
Attribute Characteristics:	Integer	Number of Attributes:	30	Date Donated	2015-03-26
Associated Tasks:	Classification	Missing Values?	N/A	Number of Web Hits:	72541

The dataset is provided as an `arff` file:

```
@relation phishing

@attribute having_IP_Address  { -1,1 }
@attribute URL_Length   { 1,0,-1 }
@attribute Shortining_Service { 1,-1 }
@attribute having_At_Symbol   { 1,-1 }
@attribute double_slash_redirecting { -1,1 }
@attribute Prefix_Suffix  { -1,1 }
@attribute having_Sub_Domain  { -1,0,1 }
@attribute SSLfinal_State  { -1,1,0 }
@attribute Domain_registeration_length { -1,1 }
@attribute Favicon { 1,-1 }
@attribute port { 1,-1 }
@attribute HTTPS_token { -1,1 }
@attribute Request_URL  { 1,-1 }
@attribute URL_of_Anchor { -1,0,1 }
@attribute Links_in_tags { 1,-1,0 }
@attribute SFH  { -1,1,0 }
@attribute Submitting_to_email { -1,1 }
@attribute Abnormal_URL { -1,1 }
@attribute Redirect   { 0,1 }
@attribute on_mouseover  { 1,-1 }
@attribute RightClick  { 1,-1 }
@attribute popUpWidnow  { 1,-1 }
@attribute Iframe { 1,-1 }
@attribute age_of_domain  { -1,1 }
@attribute DNSRecord   { -1,1 }
@attribute web_traffic  { -1,0,1 }
@attribute Page_Rank { -1,1 }
@attribute Google_Index { 1,-1 }
@attribute Links_pointing_to_page { 1,0,-1 }
@attribute Statistical_report { -1,1 }
@attribute Result  { -1,1 }
```

The following is a snapshot from the dataset:

```
@data
-1,1,1,1,-1,-1,-1,-1,-1,1,1,-1,1,-1,1,-1,-1,-1,0,1,1,1,1,-1,-1,-1,-1,1,1,-1,-1
1,1,1,1,1,-1,0,1,-1,1,1,-1,1,0,-1,-1,1,1,0,1,1,1,1,-1,-1,0,-1,1,1,1,-1
1,0,1,1,1,-1,-1,-1,-1,1,1,-1,1,0,-1,-1,-1,-1,0,1,1,1,1,1,-1,1,-1,1,0,-1,-1
1,0,1,1,1,-1,-1,-1,1,1,1,-1,-1,0,0,-1,1,1,0,1,1,1,1,-1,-1,1,-1,1,1,-1,-1
1,0,-1,1,1,-1,1,1,-1,1,1,1,1,0,0,-1,1,1,0,-1,1,-1,1,-1,-1,0,-1,1,1,1,1
-1,0,-1,1,-1,-1,1,1,-1,1,1,-1,1,0,0,-1,-1,-1,0,1,1,1,1,1,1,1,-1,1,-1,-1,1
1,0,-1,1,1,-1,-1,-1,1,1,1,1,-1,-1,0,-1,-1,-1,0,1,1,1,1,1,-1,1,-1,1,0,-1,-1
1,0,1,1,1,-1,-1,-1,1,1,1,1,-1,-1,0,-1,-1,1,1,0,1,1,1,1,-1,-1,0,-1,1,0,1,-1
1,0,-1,1,1,-1,1,1,-1,1,1,-1,1,0,1,-1,1,1,0,1,1,1,1,-1,1,1,1,0,1,1
1,1,-1,1,1,-1,-1,1,-1,1,1,1,1,0,1,-1,1,1,0,1,1,1,1,-1,0,-1,1,0,1,-1
1,1,1,1,1,-1,0,1,1,1,1,1,-1,0,0,-1,-1,-1,0,1,1,1,1,-1,1,1,1,1,-1,-1,1
1,1,-1,1,1,-1,-1,-1,-1,1,1,1,1,-1,-1,-1,-1,-1,0,1,1,1,1,-1,-1,-1,-1,1,0,-1,-1
-1,1,-1,1,-1,-1,0,0,1,1,1,-1,-1,-1,1,-1,1,1,0,-1,1,-1,1,1,-1,-1,-1,1,0,1,-1
1,1,-1,1,1,-1,0,-1,1,1,1,1,-1,-1,-1,-1,1,1,0,1,1,1,1,-1,-1,0,-1,1,1,1,-1
1,1,-1,1,1,1,-1,-1,1,1,-1,-1,1,1,-1,1,1,0,1,1,1,1,-1,1,-1,1,-1,-1,1
1,-1,-1,1,1,-1,0,0,1,1,1,1,-1,-1,0,-1,1,1,0,1,1,1,1,1,-1,-1,-1,1,0,1,-1
1,-1,-1,1,1,-1,1,1,-1,1,1,-1,1,0,-1,-1,-1,-1,0,1,1,1,1,1,-1,0,-1,1,1,-1,-1
1,1,1,1,1,-1,-1,0,1,1,-1,1,1,0,-1,-1,-1,-1,0,1,1,1,1,1,-1,-1,1,1,-1,1,-1,-1
1,1,1,1,1,-1,-1,1,1,1,-1,1,0,-1,-1,-1,-1,0,1,1,1,1,1,-1,-1,1,1,-1,-1,1
1,1,1,1,1,-1,-1,1,-1,1,1,1,1,0,0,-1,-1,-1,0,-1,-1,-1,-1,1,-1,0,-1,1,0,-1,1
1,0,-1,1,1,-1,0,1,-1,1,1,1,1,0,0,-1,-1,-1,0,-1,1,-1,1,1,-1,1,1,1,-1,1,-1,-1,1
1,0,1,1,1,-1,0,1,1,1,1,-1,-1,0,-1,-1,-1,-1,0,1,1,1,1,-1,1,1,-1,-1,-1,1,0,-1,1
1,1,1,1,1,-1,-1,-1,-1,1,1,1,-1,1,0,0,-1,1,1,0,1,1,1,1,1,1,0,-1,1,-1,1,1
1,1,1,1,1,-1,-1,1,0,-1,1,1,1,1,0,0,-1,1,1,0,1,1,1,1,1,1,1,-1,-1,-1,1,1,1
1,-1,-1,-1,1,-1,1,1,-1,1,1,1,-1,-1,0,0,-1,1,1,0,1,1,1,1,1,1,-1,-1,1,0,1,1
1,-1,1,1,1,-1,-1,0,1,1,1,1,1,1,0,-1,1,1,0,1,1,1,1,-1,1,1,-1,1,0,1,1
1,-1,1,1,1,-1,0,-1,1,1,1,-1,-1,-1,-1,-1,-1,1,-1,0,1,1,1,1,1,1,0,-1,1,-1,-1,-1,-1
1,-1,-1,1,1,1,-1,1,1,1,1,1,-1,1,0,-1,-1,-1,0,1,1,1,1,1,-1,0,-1,1,0,-1,1
1,-1,-1,1,-1,-1,1,-1,1,1,1,1,1,1,0,-1,-1,-1,0,-1,1,1,1,1,1,-1,-1,1,-1,-1,1,1,1
1,-1,1,1,1,-1,-1,-1,1,1,1,1,1,0,-1,1,1,0,1,1,1,1,-1,-1,1,1,1,0,1,1
1,-1,1,1,1,-1,-1,-1,1,-1,1,1,-1,1,0,1,-1,1,1,0,1,1,1,1,-1,-1,-1,-1,1,1,0,1,1
1,-1,1,1,1,-1,-1,1,1,-1,1,1,-1,1,0,-1,-1,-1,-1,0,-1,1,1,-1,-1,1,1,-1,1,1,1,0,-1,1
1,-1,1,1,1,1,1,1,1,-1,1,1,1,1,1,1,-1,-1,0,1,1,1,1,1,1,-1,-1,1,-1,-1,1
1,0,1,1,1,-1,-1,1,1,-1,1,1,1,1,0,1,-1,-1,-1,0,1,1,1,1,1,1,1,-1,1,0,-1,1
```

For better manipulation, we have organized the dataset into a `csv` file:

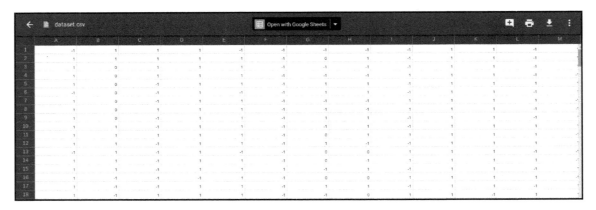

As you probably noticed from the attributes, each line of the dataset is represented in the following format – *{30 Attributes (having_IP_Address URL_Length, abnormal_URL and so on)} + {1 Attribute (Result)}*:

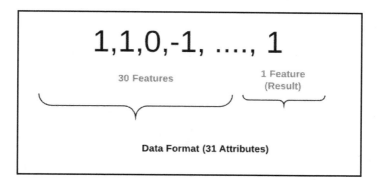

For our model, we are going to import two machine learning libraries, NumPy and scikit-learn, which we already installed in chapter 1, *Introduction to Machine Learning in Pentesting*.

Let's open the Python environment and load the required libraries:

```
>>> import numpy as np
>>> from sklearn import *
>>> from sklearn.linear_model import LogisticRegression
>>> from sklearn.metrics import accuracy_score
```

Next, load the data:

```
training_data = np.genfromtxt('dataset.csv', delimiter=',', dtype=np.int32)
```

Identify the inputs (all of the attributes, except for the last one) and the outputs (the last attribute):

```
>>> inputs = training_data[:, :-1]
>>> outputs = training_data[:, -1]
```

In the previous chapter, we discussed how we need to divide the dataset into training data and testing data:

```
training_inputs = inputs[:2000]
training_outputs = outputs[:2000]
testing_inputs = inputs[2000:]
testing_outputs = outputs[2000:]
```

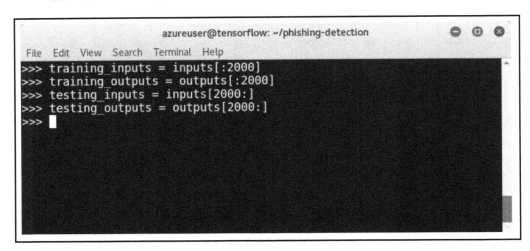

Create the scikit-learn logistic regression classifier:

```
classifier = LogisticRegression()
```

Train the classifier:

```
classifier.fit(training_inputs, training_outputs)
```

Make predictions:

```
predictions = classifier.predict(testing_inputs)
```

Let's print out the accuracy of our phishing detector model:

```
accuracy = 100.0 * accuracy_score(testing_outputs, predictions)

print ("The accuracy of your Logistic Regression on testing data is: " +
str(accuracy))
```

```
azureuser@tensorflow: ~/phishing-detection

File   Edit   View   Search   Terminal   Help
>>> classifier = LogisticRegression()
>>> classifier.fit(training_inputs, training_outputs)
LogisticRegression(C=1.0, class_weight=None, dual=False, fit_intercept=True,
          intercept_scaling=1, max_iter=100, multi_class='ovr', n_jobs=1,
          penalty='l2', random_state=None, solver='liblinear', tol=0.0001,
          verbose=0, warm_start=False)
>>> predictions = classifier.predict(testing_inputs)
>>> accuracy = 100.0 * accuracy_score(testing_outputs, predictions)
>>> print ("The accuracy of your Logistic Regression on testing data is: " + str(accuracy
))
The accuracy of your Logistic Regression on testing data is: 84.85919381557152
>>>
```

The accuracy of our model is approximately 85%. This is a good accuracy, since our model detected 85 phishing URLs out of 100. But let's try to make an even better model with decision trees, using the same data.

Phishing detection with decision trees

To build the second model, we are going to use the same machine learning libraries, so there is no need to import them again. However, we are going to import the decision tree classifier from `sklearn`:

```
>>> from sklearn import tree
```

Create the `tree.DecisionTreeClassifier()` scikit-learn classifier:

```
classifier = tree.DecisionTreeClassifier()
```

Train the model:

```
classifier.fit(training_inputs, training_outputs)
```

Compute the predictions:

```
predictions = classifier.predict(testing_inputs)
```

Calculate the accuracy:

```
accuracy = 100.0 * accuracy_score(testing_outputs, predictions)
```

Then, print out the results:

```
print ("The accuracy of your decision tree on testing data is: " +
str(accuracy))
```

The accuracy of the second model is approximately 90.4%, which is a great result, compared to the first model. We have now learned how to build two phishing detectors, using two machine learning techniques.

NLP in-depth overview

NLP is the art of analyzing and understanding human languages by machines. According to many studies, more than 75% of the used data is unstructured. Unstructured data does not have a predefined data model or not organized in a predefined manner. Emails, tweets, daily messages and even our recorded speeches are forms of unstructured data. NLP is a way for machines to analyze, understand, and derive meaning from natural language. NLP is widely used in many fields and applications, such as:

- Real-time translation
- Automatic summarization
- Sentiment analysis
- Speech recognition
- Build chatbots

Generally, there are two different components of NLP:

- **Natural Language Understanding (NLU)**: This refers to mapping input into a useful representation.
- **Natural Language Generation (NLG)**: This refers to transforming internal representations into useful representations. In other words, it is transforming data into written or spoken narrative. Written analysis for business intelligence dashboards is one of NLG applications.

Every NLP project goes through five steps. To build an NLP project the first step is identifying and analyzing the structure of words. This step involves dividing the data into paragraphs, sentences, and words. Later we analyze the words in the sentences and relationships among them. The third step involves checking the text for meaningfulness. Then, analyzing the meaning of consecutive sentences. Finally, we finish the project by the pragmatic analysis.

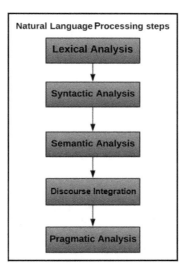

Open source NLP libraries

There are many open source Python libraries that provide the structures required to build real-world NLP applications, such as:

- Apache OpenNLP
- GATE NLP library
- Stanford NLP
- And, of course, **Natural Language Toolkit (NLTK)**

In the previous chapter, we learned how to install many open source machine learning Python libraries, including the NLTK. Let's fire up our Linux machine and try some hands-on techniques.

Open the Python terminal and import `nltk`:

```
>>> import nltk
```

Download a book type, as follows:

```
>>> nltk.download()
```

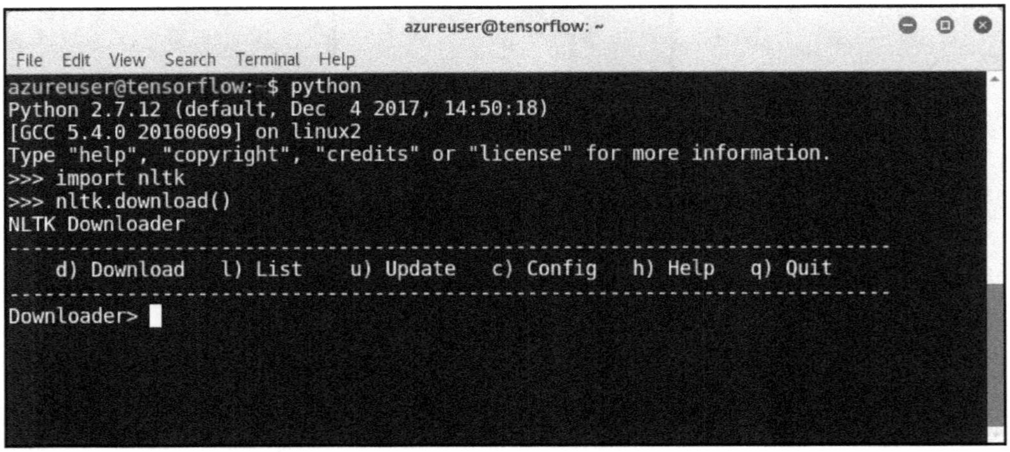

If you want to list the available resources that we already downloaded in the previous chapter, type 1:

```
                           azureuser@tensorflow: ~
File  Edit  View  Search  Terminal  Help
Packages:
  [*] abc................. Australian Broadcasting Commission 2006
  [*] alpino.............. Alpino Dutch Treebank
  [*] averaged_perceptron_tagger Averaged Perceptron Tagger
  [ ] averaged_perceptron_tagger_ru Averaged Perceptron Tagger (Russian)
  [*] basque_grammars..... Grammars for Basque
  [*] biocreative_ppi..... BioCreAtIvE (Critical Assessment of Information
                           Extraction Systems in Biology)
  [*] bllip_wsj_no_aux.... BLLIP Parser: WSJ Model
  [*] book_grammars....... Grammars from NLTK Book
  [*] brown............... Brown Corpus
  [*] brown_tei.......... Brown Corpus (TEI XML Version)
  [*] cess_cat........... CESS-CAT Treebank
  [*] cess_esp........... CESS-ESP Treebank
  [*] chat80............. Chat-80 Data Files
  [*] city_database...... City Database
```

You can also type:

```
>> from nltk.book import *
```

```
                           azureuser@tensorflow: ~
File  Edit  View  Search  Terminal  Help
Python 2.7.12 (default, Dec  4 2017, 14:50:18)
[GCC 5.4.0 20160609] on linux2
Type "help", "copyright", "credits" or "license" for more information.
>>> from nltk.book import *
*** Introductory Examples for the NLTK Book ***
Loading text1, ..., text9 and sent1, ..., sent9
Type the name of the text or sentence to view it.
Type: 'texts()' or 'sents()' to list the materials.
text1: Moby Dick by Herman Melville 1851
text2: Sense and Sensibility by Jane Austen 1811
text3: The Book of Genesis
text4: Inaugural Address Corpus
text5: Chat Corpus
text6: Monty Python and the Holy Grail
text7: Wall Street Journal
text8: Personals Corpus
text9: The Man Who Was Thursday by G . K . Chesterton 1908
>>>
```

To get text from a link, it is recommended to use the `urllib` module to crawl a website:

```
>>> from urllib import urlopen
>>> url = "http://www.URL_HERE/file.txt"
```

As a demonstration, we are going to load a text called
`Security.in.Wireless.Ad.Hoc.and.Sensor.Networks`:

```
azureuser@tensorflow: ~

File  Edit  View  Search  Terminal  Help
azureuser@tensorflow:~$ python
Python 2.7.12 (default, Dec  4 2017, 14:50:18)
[GCC 5.4.0 20160609] on linux2
Type "help", "copyright", "credits" or "license" for more information.
>>> from urllib import urlopen
>>> url = "https://archive.org/stream/TxtBook-security.in.wireless.ad.hoc.and.se
nsor.networks/Wiley.Security.in.Wireless.Ad.Hoc.and.Sensor.Networks.Mar.2009.eBo
ok-DDU_djvu.txt"
>>> raw = urlopen(url).read()
>>> len(raw)
743800
>>> raw[:50]
'<!DOCTYPE html>\n<html lang="en">\n<!-- _ _ _ _ _|'
>>>
```

We crawled the text file, and used `len` to check its length and `raw[:50]` to display some content. As you can see from the screenshot, the text contains a lot of symbols that are useless for our projects. To get only what we need, we use **tokenization**:

```
>>> tokens = nltk.word_tokenize(raw)
>>> len(tokens)
> tokens[:10]
```

To summarize what we learned in the previous section, we saw how to download a web page, tokenize the text, and normalize the words.

Spam detection with NLTK

Now it is time to build our spam detector using the NLTK. The principle of this type of classifier is simple; we need to detect the words used by spammers. We are going to build a spam/non-spam binary classifier using Python and the `nltk` library, to detect whether or not an email is spam. First, we need to import the library as usual:

```
>>> import nltk
```

We need to load data and feed our model with an emails dataset. To achieve that, we can use the dataset delivered by the **Internet CONtent FIltering Group**. You can visit the website at `https://labs-repos.iit.demokritos.gr/skel/i-config/`:

Basically, the website provides four datasets:

- Ling-spam
- PU1
- PU123A
- Enron-spam

For our project, we are going to use the Enron-spam dataset:

Name	Last modified	Size	Description
Parent Directory		-	
enron1.tar.gz	22-Jun-2006 16:24	1.7M	
enron2.tar.gz	22-Jun-2006 16:24	2.8M	
enron3.tar.gz	22-Jun-2006 16:24	4.4M	
enron4.tar.gz	22-Jun-2006 16:24	2.4M	
enron5.tar.gz	22-Jun-2006 16:24	2.3M	
enron6.tar.gz	22-Jun-2006 16:24	3.0M	

Let's download the dataset using the `wget` command:

```
                          azureuser@tensorflow: ~/spam_filter
File  Edit  View  Search  Terminal  Help
azureuser@tensorflow:~/spam_filter$ wget --no-check-certificate https://labs-repos.iit.demokritos.
gr/skel/i-config/downloads/enron-spam/preprocessed/enron1.tar.gz
--2018-04-10 15:47:47--  https://labs-repos.iit.demokritos.gr/skel/i-config/downloads/enron-spam/p
reprocessed/enron1.tar.gz
Resolving labs-repos.iit.demokritos.gr (labs-repos.iit.demokritos.gr)... 143.233.226.4
Connecting to labs-repos.iit.demokritos.gr (labs-repos.iit.demokritos.gr)|143.233.226.4|:443... co
nnected.
WARNING: cannot verify labs-repos.iit.demokritos.gr's certificate, issued by 'CN=TERENA SSL CA 3,0
=TERENA,L=Amsterdam,ST=Noord-Holland,C=NL':
  Unable to locally verify the issuer's authority.
WARNING: no certificate subject alternative name matches
        requested host name 'labs-repos.iit.demokritos.gr'.
HTTP request sent, awaiting response... 200 OK
Length: 1802573 (1.7M) [application/x-gzip]
Saving to: 'enron1.tar.gz'
```

Extract the `tar.gz` file by using the `tar -xzf enron1.tar.gz` command:

```
                      azureuser@tensorflow: ~/spam_filter/enron1
File  Edit  View  Search  Terminal  Help
azureuser@tensorflow:~/spam_filter$ ls
enron1  enron1.tar.gz
azureuser@tensorflow:~/spam_filter$ cd enron1
azureuser@tensorflow:~/spam_filter/enron1$ ls
ham  spam  Summary.txt
azureuser@tensorflow:~/spam_filter/enron1$ ls spam
0006.2003-12-18.GP.spam.txt  2662.2004-10-29.GP.spam.txt
0008.2003-12-18.GP.spam.txt  2668.2004-10-29.GP.spam.txt
0017.2003-12-18.GP.spam.txt  2670.2004-10-30.GP.spam.txt
0018.2003-12-18.GP.spam.txt  2673.2004-10-30.GP.spam.txt
0026.2003-12-18.GP.spam.txt  2677.2004-10-30.GP.spam.txt
0032.2003-12-19.GP.spam.txt  2680.2004-10-30.GP.spam.txt
0040.2003-12-19.GP.spam.txt  2681.2004-10-31.GP.spam.txt
0041.2003-12-19.GP.spam.txt  2682.2004-10-31.GP.spam.txt
0046.2003-12-20.GP.spam.txt  2686.2004-10-31.GP.spam.txt
0052.2003-12-20.GP.spam.txt  2692.2004-10-31.GP.spam.txt
0054.2003-12-21.GP.spam.txt  2697.2004-10-31.GP.spam.txt
0058.2003-12-21.GP.spam.txt  2698.2004-10-31.GP.spam.txt
```

Shuffle the `cp spam/* emails && cp ham/* emails` object:

```
2577.2000-10-18.farmer.ham.txt   5163.2005-09-06.GP.spam.txt
2578.2000-10-18.farmer.ham.txt   5164.2005-09-06.GP.spam.txt
2579.2000-10-18.farmer.ham.txt   5165.2002-01-09.farmer.ham.txt
2580.2004-10-22.GP.spam.txt      5166.2002-01-09.farmer.ham.txt
2581.2004-10-23.GP.spam.txt      5167.2005-09-06.GP.spam.txt
2582.2000-10-18.farmer.ham.txt   5168.2002-01-10.farmer.ham.txt
2583.2004-10-23.GP.spam.txt      5169.2002-01-11.farmer.ham.txt
2584.2000-10-18.farmer.ham.txt   5170.2005-09-06.GP.spam.txt
2585.2004-10-24.GP.spam.txt      5171.2005-09-06.GP.spam.txt
2586.2000-10-18.farmer.ham.txt   5172.2002-01-11.farmer.ham.txt
```

To shuffle the emails, let's write a small Python script, `Shuffle.py`, to do the job:

```python
import os
import random
#initiate a list called emails_list
emails_list = []
Directory = '/home/azureuser/spam_filter/enron1/emails/'
Dir_list  = os.listdir(Directory)
for file in Dir_list:
    f = open(Directory + file, 'r')
    emails_list.append(f.read())
f.close()
```

Just change the directory variable, and it will shuffle the files:

After preparing the dataset, you should be aware that, as we learned previously, we need to `tokenize` the emails:

```
>> from nltk import word_tokenize
```

Also, we need to perform another step, called lemmatizing. Lemmatizing connects words that have different forms, like hacker/hackers and is/are. We need to import `WordNetLemmatizer`:

```
>>> from nltk import WordNetLemmatizer
```

Create a sentence for the demonstration, and print out the result of the lemmatizer:

```
>>> [lemmatizer.lemmatize(word.lower()) for word in
word_tokenize(unicode(sentence, errors='ignore'))]
```

Then, we need to remove `stopwords`, such as `of`, `is`, `the`, and so on:

```
from nltk.corpus import stopwords
stop = stopwords.words('english')
```

To process the email, a function called `Process` must be created, to `lemmatize` and `tokenize` our dataset:

```
def Process(data):
    lemmatizer = WordNetLemmatizer()
    return [lemmatizer.lemmatize(word.lower()) for word in
word_tokenize(unicode(sentence,    errors='ignore'))]
```

The second step is feature extraction, by reading the emails' words:

```
from collections import Counter
def Features_Extraction(text, setting):
    if setting=='bow':
# Bow means   bag-of-words
        return {word: count for word, count in
Counter(Process(text)).items() if not word in stop}
    else:
        return {word: True for word in Process(text) if not word in stop}
```

Extract the features:

```
features = [(Features_Extraction(email, 'bow'), label) for (email, label)
in emails]
```

Now, let's define training the model Python function:

```
def training_Model (Features, samples):
    Size = int(len(Features) * samples)
    training , testing = Features[:Size], Features[Size:]
    print ('Training = ' + str(len(training)) + ' emails')
    print ('Testing = ' + str(len(testing)) + ' emails')
```

As a classification algorithm, we are going to use `NaiveBayesClassifier`:

```
from nltk import NaiveBayesClassifier, classify
classifier = NaiveBayesClassifier.train(training)
```

Finally, we define the evaluation Python function:

```
def evaluate(training, tesing, classifier):
    print ('Training Accuracy is ' + str(classify.accuracy(classifier,
train_set)))
    print ('Testing Accuracy i ' + str(classify.accuracy(classifier,
test_set)))
```

```
Training Accuracy is 0.960599468214
Testing Accuracy is 0.946859903382
Most Informative Features
            forwarded = True              ham : spam   =    197.3 : 1.0
         prescription = True             spam : ham    =    132.4 : 1.0
                  nom = True              ham : spam   =    121.0 : 1.0
                  ect = True              ham : spam   =    115.3 : 1.0
                 pain = True             spam : ham    =    109.1 : 1.0
                meter = True              ham : spam   =    108.3 : 1.0
                 2005 = True             spam : ham    =     92.5 : 1.0
                 spam = True             spam : ham    =     92.5 : 1.0
           nomination = True              ham : spam   =     92.2 : 1.0
               health = True             spam : ham    =     87.5 : 1.0
                cheap = True             spam : ham    =     85.8 : 1.0
               dealer = True             spam : ham    =     84.1 : 1.0
                  sex = True             spam : ham    =     77.5 : 1.0
                   ex = True             spam : ham    =     75.8 : 1.0
                differ = True            spam : ham    =     74.1 : 1.0
                 2001 = True              ham : spam   =     72.7 : 1.0
               weight = True             spam : ham    =     72.5 : 1.0
             creative = True             spam : ham    =     69.1 : 1.0
               reader = True             spam : ham    =     69.1 : 1.0
           subscriber = True             spam : ham    =     67.5 : 1.0
>>> 
```

Summary

In this chapter, we learned to detect phishing attempts by building three different projects from scratch. First, we discovered how to develop a phishing detector using two different machine learning techniques, thanks to cutting-edge Python machine learning libraries. The third project was a spam filter, based on NLP and Naive Bayes classification. In the next chapter, we will build various projects to detect malware, using different techniques and Python machine learning libraries.

Questions

We hope it was easy to go through this chapter. Now, as usual, it is practice time. Your job is to try building your own spam detection system. We will guide you through the questions.

In this chapter's GitHub repository, you will find a dataset collected from research done by Androutsopoulos, J. Koutsias, K.V. Chandrinos, George Paliouras, and C.D. Spyropoulos: *An Evaluation of Naive Bayesian Anti-Spam Filtering. Proceedings of the workshop on Machine Learning in the New Information Age, G. Potamias, V. Moustakis and M. van Someren (eds.), 11th European Conference on Machine Learning, Barcelona, Spain, pp. 9-17, 2000.*

You can now prepare the data:

1. The following are some text-cleaning tasks to perform:
   - Clean your texts of stopwords, digits, and punctuation marks.
   - Perform lemmatization.
2. Create a word dictionary, including their frequencies.

 In email texts, you will notice that the first line is the subject of the email and the third line is the body of the email (we only need the email bodies).

3. Remove the non-words from the dictionary.
4. Extract the features from the data.
5. Prepare the feature vectors and their labels.
6. Train the model with a linear support vector machine classifier.
7. Print out the confusion matrix of your model.

3
Malware Detection with API Calls and PE Headers

Some of the most annoying threats in information security are malicious programs. Every day, we hear news about data breaches and cyber attacks with malware. Attackers are enhancing their development skills and building new malware that are able to bypass company safeguards and AV-products. This chapter will introduce some new techniques and solutions for defeating malware, using cutting-edge data science, Python libraries, and machine learning algorithms.

In this chapter, we will cover:

- Malware analysis approaches
- Machine learning aided malware analysis techniques, with practical, real-world Python projects

Technical requirements

In this chapter, we will use the same Python libraries that we already installed. We are going to use those libraries during most of the chapters in this book. That is why we used the first chapter to teach you how to install all of the required libraries.

You will find all of the codes discussed, in addition to some other useful scripts, in the repository at https://github.com/PacktPublishing/Mastering-Machine-Learning-for-Penetration-Testing/tree/master/Chapter03.

Malware overview

Malware are malicious pieces of software that are designed to infiltrate and damage information systems without the users' consent. The term *malware* covers a lot of categories. There are many different types of malware:

- Viruses
- Ransomware
- Worms
- Trojans
- Backdoor
- Spyware
- Keyloggers
- Adware, bots, and rootkits

Malware analysis

Your job, as a malware analyst, is to discover exactly what happened to a system, and to make sure that the machines damaged by malicious software are isolated from the organization's network. In order to perform malware analysis, we need to follow specific operations and approaches. When it comes to malware analysis, we have to perform three techniques: static malware analysis, dynamic malware analysis, and memory malware analysis. We are going to look at them one by one.

Static malware analysis

The first step in malware analysis is gathering all of the information about the malware. Static analysis is the art of collecting all of the available information about the malicious binary, using different techniques and utilities. In this phase, the analyst examines the malware without really executing it. Some common static malware analysis methods are as follows:

- **Online antivirus scanning**: Scanning the suspicious file using an online scanner is a good way to check the file, thanks to online environments that give you the ability to scan the file using many antivirus products. The most well known online scanner is VirusTotal. If you want to scan a file, just visit `https://www.virustotal.com/#/home/upload` and upload the file:

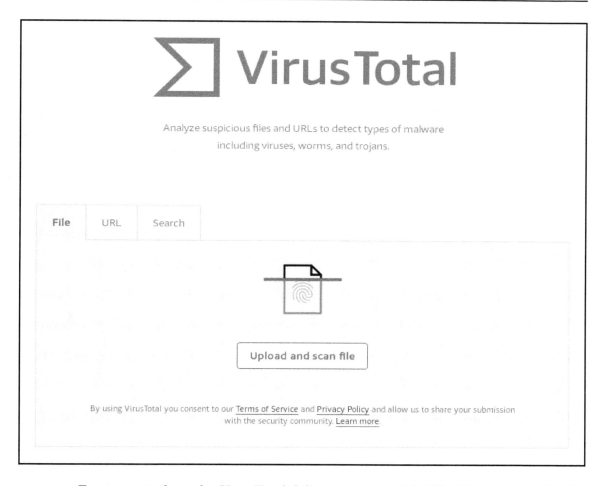

To automate the tasks, VirusTotal delivers some useful APIs. Thus, you can build your own Python script with a few lines:

Python

VirusTotal public API version 2.0 implementation in Python 2.x by Chris Clark and Adam Meyers.

VirusTotal public API version 2.0 implementation in Python 2.x by Gawen Arab.

VirusTotal public API version 2.0 implementation in Python 2.x by @techno_vikiing.

Single and bulk lookups with VirusTotal public API version 2.0 by Claudio Guarnieri.

To scan `file.exe`, you could use the following code snippet from VirusTotal:

```
import requests
url = 'https://www.virustotal.com/vtapi/v2/file/scan'
params = {'apikey': '<apikey>'}
files = {'file': ('myfile.exe', open('myfile.exe', 'rb'))}
response = requests.post(url, files=files, params=params)
print(response.json())
```

To obtain a key, just create a VirusTotal community account.

- **Hashing**: This is a technique to identify files. Each hashed file has a unique hash. The most commonly used hash functions are MD5 and SHA256.
- **Strings**: These are also great sources of information. Extracting strings from the malicious program will give us juicy information about the malware. Some strings include URIs, URLs, error messages, and comments.

Dynamic malware analysis

After collecting information about malware, you should run it in an isolated and secure environment. Generally, these environments are called **malware analysis sandboxes**. Sandboxes are loaded with analysis and monitoring tools to gather information about the malware while it is running. Malware analysts can collect the following information, and more:

- TCP connections
- DNS summaries
- Malware behaviors
- System calls

Memory malware analysis

Years ago, using the two previous techniques was enough to analyze malware, but attackers are now using new, more complicated techniques to avoid detection. I bet that you have heard about fileless malware. Memory malware analysis is needed to detect the new wave of malware. Memory malware analysis occurs by analyzing memory dumps collected from infected machines. In order to perform memory analysis, the analyst first needs to acquire memory (dumping memory), and can analyze it later by using many utilities and techniques.

One of the most used frameworks is the volatility framework. If you have installed a Kali Linux distribution, you can use volatility directly on your machine without installing it. The following screenshot was taken from a Kali Linux built-in volatility framework:

```
                              root@kali: /home/ghost                        ⊖  ⊡  ⊗
 File  Edit  View  Search  Terminal  Help
root@kali:/home/ghost# sudo volatility -h
Volatility Foundation Volatility Framework 2.5
Usage: Volatility - A memory forensics analysis platform.

Options:
  -h, --help              list all available options and their default values.
                          Default values may be set in the configuration file
                          (/etc/volatilityrc)
  --conf-file=/root/.volatilityrc
                          User based configuration file
  -d, --debug             Debug volatility
  --plugins=PLUGINS       Additional plugin directories to use (colon separated)
  --info                  Print information about all registered objects
  --cache-directory=/root/.cache/volatility
                          Directory where cache files are stored
  --cache                 Use caching
  --tz=TZ                 Sets the (Olson) timezone for displaying timestamps
                          using pytz (if installed) or tzset
  -f FILENAME, --filename=FILENAME
                          Filename to use when opening an image
  --profile=WinXPSP2x86
                          Name of the profile to load (use --info to see a list
                          of supported profiles)
  -l LOCATION, --location=LOCATION
                          A URN location from which to load an address space
  -w, --write             Enable write support
  --dtb=DTB               DTB Address
```

Volatility helps analysts to collect information from memory dumps, including the following, and more:

- Bash history
- API hooks
- Network information
- Kernel-loaded modules

Evasion techniques

Attackers and malware developers are continuously coming up with new techniques and methods to avoid detection. Some of the most common techniques are:

- **Obfuscation**: This is the practice of making the malware more difficult to detect or analyze. Dead-code insertion, register reassignment, and crypting are three obfuscation techniques.

- **Binding**: This is the practice of binding a malware with a legitimate file, resulting in a single executable.
- **Packing**: A packer, sometimes called a **self-extracting archive**, is a software that unpacks itself in memory when the *packed file* is executed.

Portable Executable format files

Portable Executable (PE) files are file formats for executables, DDLs, and object codes used in 32-bit and 64-bit versions of Windows. They contain many useful pieces of information for malware analysts, including imports, exports, time-date stamps, subsystems, sections, and resources. The following is the basic structure of a PE file:

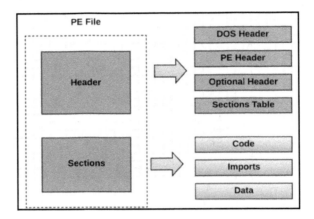

Some of the components of a PE file are as follows:

- **DOS Header**: This starts with the first 64 bytes of every PE file, so DOS can validate the executable and can run it in the DOS stub mode.
- **PE Header**: This contains information, including the location and size of the code.
- **PE Sections**: They contain the main contents of the file.

To explore the PE header's information, you can use many tools, such as PE EXPLORER, PEview, and PEstudio.

Machine learning malware detection using PE headers

To train our machine learning models to find malware datasets, there are a lot of publicly available sources for data scientists and malware analysts. For example, the following websites give security researchers and machine learning enthusiasts the ability to download many different malware samples:

- **Malware-Traffic-Analysis**: `https://www.malware-traffic-analysis.net/`
- **Kaggle Malware Families**: `https://www.kaggle.com/c/malware-classification`
- **VX Heaven**: `http://83.133.184.251/virensimulation.org/index.html`
- **VirusTotal**: `https://www.virustotal.com`
- **VirusShare**: `https://virusshare.com`

To work with PE files, I highly recommend using an amazing Python library called `pefile`. `pefile` gives you the ability to inspect headers, analyze sections, and retrieve data, in addition to other capabilities, like packer detection and PEiD signature generation. You can check out the GitHub project at `https://github.com/erocarrera/pefile`.

You can also install it with PIP, like we did with the other machine learning libraries:

```
# pip install pefile
```

Now we installed `pefile` successfully:

Let's start to build our first malware classifier. For this model, we are going to use three different techniques:

- Random forests
- Gradient-boosting classification
- AdaBoost classification

As you may have noticed from the classification algorithms in this book, we are trying to use many different techniques. In some cases, you can use one of the previously discussed algorithms, but I am trying to use different techniques in every chapter, so that you can acquire a clear understanding of how to use each machine learning technique.

By now, you are aware that the first step to building a machine learning model (after studying the project needs and requirements, of course) is downloading a dataset. In this section, we are going to download a malware dataset delivered by a security blogger, Prateek Lalwani. The malware dataset contains features extracted from the following:

- 41,323 Windows binaries (executables .exe and .dlls), as legitimate files.
- 96,724 malware files downloaded from the VirusShare website. So, the dataset contains 138,048 lines, in total.

The dataset is divided as follows:

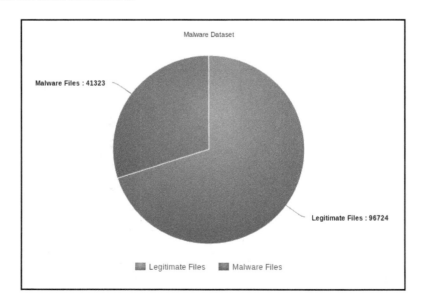

Let's start by loading the malware dataset using the `pandas` Python library:

```
import pandas as pd
MalwareDataset = pd.read_csv('MalwareData.csv', sep='|')
Legit = MalwareDataset[0:41323].drop(['legitimate'], axis=1)
Malware = MalwareDataset[41323::].drop(['legitimate'], axis=1)
```

```
azureuser@tensorflow: ~/Chapter3-Malware-classification
File  Edit  View  Search  Terminal  Help
azureuser@tensorflow:~/Chapter3-Malware-classification$ python
Python 2.7.12 (default, Dec  4 2017, 14:50:18)
[GCC 5.4.0 20160609] on linux2
Type "help", "copyright", "credits" or "license" for more information.
>>> import pandas as pd
>>> MalwareDataset = pd.read_csv('MalwareData.csv', sep='|')
>>> Legit = MalwareDataset[0:41323].drop(['legitimate'], axis=1)
>>> Malware = MalwareDataset[41323::].drop(['legitimate'], axis=1)
>>>
```

To make sure that the dataset has loaded properly, let's print the number of important features:

```
print('The Number of important features is  %i \n' % Legit.shape[1])
```

`The Number of important features is 56` will be the resulting line:

```
root@tensorflow: ~/Chapter3-Malware-classification
File  Edit  View  Search  Terminal  Help
>>> print('The Number of important features is  %i \n' % Legit.shape[1])
The Number of important features is  56

>>>
```

To improve the estimators' accuracy scores, we are going to use the `sklearn.feature_selection` module. This module is used in feature selection or dimensionality reduction in the dataset.

To compute the features' importance, in our case, we are going to use tree-based feature selection. Load the `sklearn.feature_selection` module:

```
import sklearn
from sklearn.feature_selection import SelectFromModel
from sklearn.ensemble import ExtraTreesClassifier
from sklearn.model_selection import train_test_split
from sklearn import cross_validation

Data = MalwareDataset.drop(['Name', 'md5', 'legitimate'], axis=1).values
Target = MalwareDataset['legitimate'].values
FeatSelect =  sklearn.ensemble.ExtraTreesClassifier().fit(Data, Target)
Model = SelectFromModel(FeatSelect, prefit=True)
Data_new = Model.transform(Data)
print (Data.shape)
print (Data_new.shape)
```

So, the algorithms has selected nine important features for us. To print them out, use the following commands:

```
Features = Data_new.shape[1]
Index =
np.argsort(ske.ExtraTreesClassifier().fit(Data,Target).feature_importances_
)[::-1][:Features]
for feat  in range(Features):
print(MalwareDataset.columns[2+index[feat]])
```

The most important features are as follows:

```
...
1. feature Characteristics (0.157282)
2. feature Machine (0.133113)
3. feature ResourcesMinEntropy (0.125373)
4. feature SectionsMaxEntropy (0.086533)
5. feature VersionInformationSize (0.073434)
6. feature Subsystem (0.060376)
7. feature DllCharacteristics (0.056196)
8. feature ResourcesMaxEntropy (0.048888)
9. feature ImageBase (0.037234)
10. feature SizeOfOptionalHeader (0.029881)
11. feature MajorSubsystemVersion (0.027777)
>>>
```

Now, it is time to train our model with a random forest classifier. Don't forget to split the dataset, like we learned previously:

```python
Legit_Train, Legit_Test, Malware_Train, Malware_Test =
cross_validation.train_test_split(Data_new, Target ,test_size=0.2)
clf =  sklearn.ensemble.RandomForestClassifier(n_estimators=50)
clf.fit(Legit_Train, Malware_Train)
score = clf.score(Legit_Test, Malware_Test)
```

```
azureuser@tensorflow: ~/Chapter3-Malware-classification

File  Edit  View  Search  Terminal  Help
>>> clf = sklearn.ensemble.RandomForestClassifier(n_estimators=50)
>>> Legit_Train, Legit_Test, Malware_Train, Malware_Test = cross_validation.train_t
est_split(Data_new, Target ,test_size=0.2)
>>> clf.fit(Legit_Train, Malware_Train)
RandomForestClassifier(bootstrap=True, class_weight=None, criterion='gini',
            max_depth=None, max_features='auto', max_leaf_nodes=None,
            min_impurity_decrease=0.0, min_impurity_split=None,
            min_samples_leaf=1, min_samples_split=2,
            min_weight_fraction_leaf=0.0, n_estimators=50, n_jobs=1,
            oob_score=False, random_state=None, verbose=0,
            warm_start=False)
>>> score = clf.score(Legit_Test, Malware_Test)
>>>
```

Let's look at the final result:

```
print("The score of Random Forest Algorithm is," score*100))
```

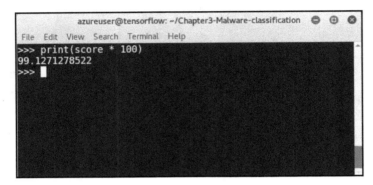

The score seems very promising. This model detected malware with a 99% success rate, which is a great result. To obtain more information about the `False positive` and `False negative` rates of our malware classifier, import the scikit-learn `confusion_matrix` module:

```
from sklearn.metrics import confusion_matrix
```

Add the following lines:

```
Result = clf.predict(Legit_Test)
CM = confusion_matrix(Malware_Test, Result)
print("False positive rate : %f %%" % ((CM[0][1] / float(sum(CM[0])))*100))
print('False negative rate : %f %%' % ( (CM[1][0] /
float(sum(CM[1]))*100)))
```

The `False positive rate` is 0.6%, and the `False negative rate` is 1.4%.

To train the model with another classifier, redo the previous steps, but instead of choosing the random forest classifier, select a machine learning algorithm. For example, I am going to select gradient-boosting:

```
Clf = sklearn.ensemble.GradientBoostingClassifier(n_estimators=50)
Clf.fit(Legit_Train, Malware_Train)
Score = Clf.score(Legit_Test, Malware_Test)
```

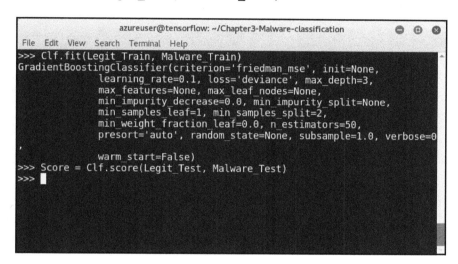

Let's check the second score:

```
print ("The Model score using Gradient Boosting is", Score * 100)
```

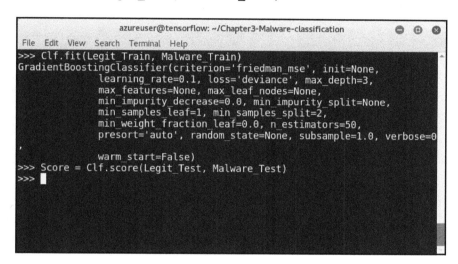

This has a 98.8% detection rate. The following is the score using the AdaBoost classifier:

```
Classifiers =
{ "RandomForest": ske.RandomForestClassifier(n_estimators=50),
  "GradientBoosting": ske.GradientBoostingClassifier(n_estimators=50),
  "AdaBoost": ske.AdaBoostClassifier(n_estimators=100),}


for Classif in Classifiers:
clf = Classifiers[Classif]
clf.fit(Legit_Train,Malware_Train)
score = clf.score(Legit_test, Malware_test)
print("%s : %f %%" % (Classif, score*100))
```

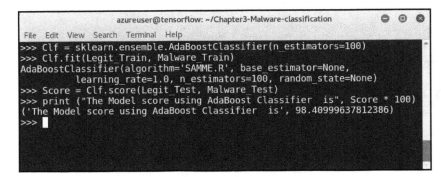

Machine learning malware detection using API calls

Analyzing malware with API calls plays a huge role in malware analysis. Thus, APIs can give malware analysts an idea about malware behavior, especially when basic, static analysis wasn't successful due to obfuscation techniques (like packers, crypters, and protectors). Malware analysts can gain an understanding of how a malicious file works by studying API calls. There are many online tools that will give you the ability to analyze malware in a secure environment. Those utilities and environments are called sandboxes. Malware that is detected is identified by a hash function (MD5 or SHA256). Malware analysts use hashing to sign a file. For example, the following APIs were taken from the report of an online malware scan with `https://www.hybrid-analysis.com`.

These are some details about the malware "PE32 executable (GUI) Intel 80386, for MS Windows". Its hash is:

4c510779ab6a58a3bdbbe8d5f3ec568fcf33df81b0f1a5bdacabf78a9c62f492

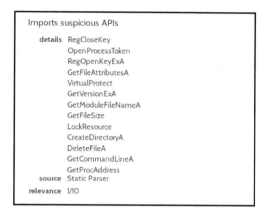

According to the Microsoft website, https://msdn.microsoft.com/, GetProcAddress retrieves the address of an exported function or variable from the specified **dynamic-link library (DLL)**. So, if you want to learn more about the other calls, just go to the Microsoft developer network and search for the API call functions:

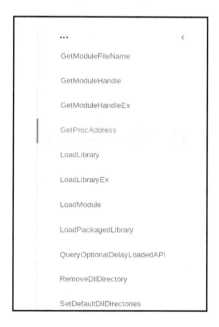

The report includes a full summary of the findings, not only the API calls. It includes:

- General information
- Malicious indicators
- Unusual characteristics
- Anti-detection/stealthiness
- Anti-reverse engineering
- Network-related information

The following are pieces of information about the scanned malware. We discussed most of the required findings (static analysis artifacts: size, type and so on) previously:

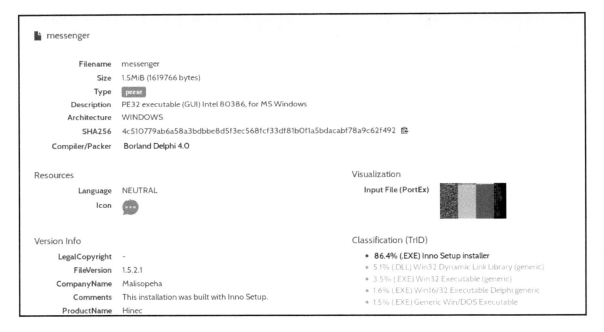

For our second malware classifier, we are going to use API calls to build a machine learning malware detector. To extract APIs from malware binaries, the malware analyst needs to go through well-defined steps:

1. Malware unpacking
2. Assembly program retrieving
3. API call extraction
4. Analyzing the API calls, using the official Microsoft website

You can categorize malware behaviors into groups. For example, the University of Ballarat categorized API calls into six categories in the article, *Towards Understanding Malware Behavior by the Extraction of API Calls*. You can use it to analyze your findings:

Behaviour	Malware Category	API Function Calls
Behaviour 1	Search Files to Infect	FindClose, FindFirstFile, FindFirstFileEx, FindFirstFileName, TransactedW, FindFirstFileNameW, FindFirstFileTransacted, FindFirstStream, TransactedW, FindFirstStreamW, FindNextFile, FindNextFileNameW, FindNextStreamW, SearchPath.
Behaviour 2	Copy/Delete Files	CloseHandle, CopyFile, CopyFileEx, CopyFileTransacted, CreateFile, CreateFileTransacted, CreateHardLink, CreateHardLink, Transacted, CreateSymbolicLink, CreateSymbolic, LinkTransacted, DeleteFile, DeleteFileTransacted.
Behaviour 3	Get File Information	GetBinaryType, GetCompressed, FileSize, GetCompressedFile, SizeTransacted, GetFileAttributes, GetFileAttributesEx, GetFileAttributes, Transacted, GetFileBandwidth, Reservation, GetFileInformation, ByHandle, GetFileInformation, ByHandleEx, GetFileSize, GetFileSizeEx, GetFileType, GetFinalPathName, ByHandle, GetFullPathName, GetFullPathName, Transacted, GetLongPathName, GetLongPathName, Transacted, GetShortPathName, GetTempFileName, GetTempPath.
Behaviour 4	Move Files	MoveFile, MoveFileEx, MoveFileTransacted, MoveFileWithProgress.
Behaviour 5	Read/Write Files	OpenFile, OpenFileById, ReOpenFile, ReplaceFile, WriteFile, CreateFile, CloseHandle.
Behaviour 6	Change File Attributes	SetFileApisToANSI, SetFileApisToOEM, SetFileAttributes, SetFileAttributesTransacted, SetFileBandwidthReservation, SetFileInformationByHandle, SetFileShortName, SetFileValidData

As a demonstration, let's build an Android malware detection project using a support vector machine learning algorithm fed by API calls dataset. This chapter's GitHub folder contains a prepared dataset to build our model:

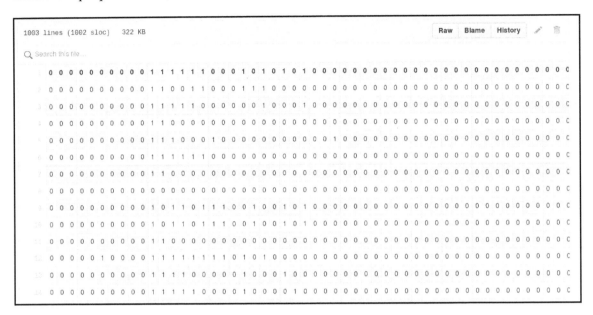

Before building the model, we need to import some useful modules:

```
>>> from sklearn.feature_selection import mutual_info_classif
>>> from sklearn import preprocessing
>>> import numpy as np
>>> from sklearn.svm import SVC, LinearSVC
>>> from sklearn import svm
>>> import csv
>>> import random
```

First, let's pre-process our CSV file (`Android_Feats.csv`):

```
>>> PRatio = 0.7
>>> Dataset =  open('Android_Feats.csv')
>>> Reader = csv.reader(Dataset)
>>> Data = list(Reader)
>>> Data = random.sample(Data, len(Data))
>>> Data = np.array(Data)
> Dataset.close()
```

Identify the data and the labels in the file using NumPy:

```
>>> cols = np.shape(Data)[1]
>>> Y = Data[:,cols-1]
>>> Y = np.array(Y)
>>> Y = np.ravel(Y,order='C')
>>> X = Data[:,:cols-1]
>>> X = X.astype(np.float)
>>> X = preprocessing.scale(X)
```

```
azureuser@tensorflow: ~/Chapter3-Malware-classification          ⊖ ⊡ ⊗
File  Edit  View  Search  Terminal  Help
>>> cols = np.shape(Data)[1]
>>> Y = Data[:,cols-1]
>>> Y = np.array(Y)
>>> Y = np.ravel(Y,order='C')
>>> X = Data[:,:cols-1]
>>> X = X.astype(np.float)
>>> X = preprocessing.scale(X)
>>> ▮
```

By now, the processing phase is done. As seen previously, we need to extract the most important features, because computing all of the available features would be a heavy task:

```
Features = [i.strip() for i in open("Android_Feats.csv").readlines()]
Features = np.array(Features)
MI= mutual_info_classif(X,Y)
Featureind = sorted(range(len(MI)), key=lambda i: MI[i], reverse=True)[:50]
SelectFeats = Features[Featureind]
```

```
azureuser@tensorflow: ~/Chapter3-Malware-classification          ⊖ ⊡ ⊗
File  Edit  View  Search  Terminal  Help

>>> Features = [i.strip() for i in open("Android_Feats.csv").readlines()]
>>> Features = np.array(Features)
>>> MI= mutual_info_classif(X,Y)
>>> Featureind = sorted(range(len(MI)), key=lambda i: MI[i], reverse=True)[:50]
>>> SelectFeats = Features[Featureind]
>>> ▮
```

Now, divide the dataset (data and labels) into training and testing sets:

```
PRows = int(PRatio*len(Data))
TrainD = X[:PRows,Featureind]
TrainL = Y[:PRows]
TestD = X[PRows:,Featureind]
TestL = Y[PRows:]
```

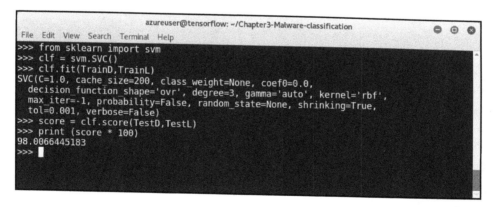

The feature selection has been successfully completed. To train the model, we are going to use the support vector machine classifier:

```
>>> clf = svm.SVC()
>>> clf.fit(TrainD,TrainL)
>>> score = clf.score(TestD,TestL)
>>> print (score * 100)
```

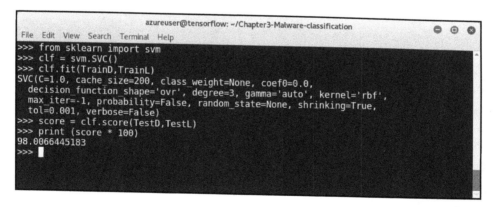

Voila! The accuracy of our new model is 98%, which is a great detection rate.

Summary

Malware is one of the most prevalent cyber threats haunting the security of modern organizations. Black hat hackers are constantly improving; hence, classic detection techniques are obsolete, and AV products are often unable to detect advanced persistent threats. That is why machine learning techniques can help us to detect malware.

In this chapter, we learned how to build malware classifiers, using many machine learning algorithms and open source Python libraries. The next chapter will teach us how to build more robust systems to detect malware, using the same algorithm used by the human mind. We are going to learn how to use deep learning to detect malware , using the same Python libraries used throughout this book.

Questions

You are now able to build a machine learning model. Let's practice, putting our new skills to the test. In this chapter's GitHub repository, you will find a dataset that contains information about Android malware samples. Now you need to build your own model, following these instructions.

In the `Chapter3-Practice` GitHub repository, you will find a dataset that contains the feature vectors of more than 11,000 benign and malicious Android applications:

1. Load the dataset using the `pandas` python library, and this time, add the `low_memory=False` parameter. Search for what that parameter does.
2. Prepare the data that will be used for training.
3. Split the data with the `test_size=0.33` parameter.
4. Create a set of classifiers that contains `DecisionTreeClassifier()`, `RandomForestClassifier(n_estimators=100)`, and `AdaBoostClassifier()`.
5. What is an `AdaBoostClassifier()`?
6. Train the model using the three classifiers and print out the metrics of every classifier.

Further reading

For more information, check out the following log posts and documents:

- PE Format (Windows): https://msdn.microsoft.com/en-us/library/windows/desktop/ms680547(v=vs.85).aspx
- *Malware Analysis: An Introduction*: https://www.sans.org/reading-room/whitepapers/malicious/malware-analysis-introduction-2103

- VirusTotal documentation: https://www.virustotal.com/en/documentation/

Malware Detection with Deep Learning

The human mind is a fascinating entity. The power of our subconscious and unconscious mind is incredible. What makes this power real is our ability to continuously self-learn and adapt quickly. This amazing gift of nature can calculate billions of tasks before you even realize what it does. For decades, scientists have been trying to build machines that are able to do simultaneous tasks like the human mind does—in other words, systems that are able to perform a huge number of tasks efficiently and at incredible speeds. A subfield of machine learning called **Deep Learning (DL)** arose to help us build algorithms that work like the human mind and are inspired by its structure. Information security professionals are also intrigued by such techniques, as they have provided promising results in defending against major cyber threats and attacks. One of the best-suited candidates for the implementation of DL is malware analysis.

In this chapter, we are going to discover:

- Artificial neural networks: an in-depth overview
- How to build your first neural network with Python
- How to build a malware detector with multi-layer perceptrons
- Malware visualization techniques and how to build a malware classifier with convolutional neural networks

Technical requirements

Basically, in this chapter, we are going to use the same Python libraries that we have already installed. Generally, we are going to use those libraries during most chapters of the book. So, we spent the first chapter teaching you how to install all the required libraries that we are going to use in most chapters and projects. Find the code files at this link: `https://github.com/PacktPublishing/Mastering-Machine-Learning-for-Penetration-Testing/tree/master/Chapter04`.

Artificial neural network overview

Our brains perform many complex functions in the blink of an eye. Thus, in order to build algorithms that perform and learn using the same techniques as the human mind, it is essential for us to learn how the brain works. By acquiring a fair understanding about how the human mind functions, we will have better understanding of deep learning. The three major distinctive mind functions are:

- Thinking (analyzing, comparing, and judging)
- Feeling (happiness, sadness, and excitement)
- Wanting (motives, desires, and goals)

These three functions are continuously interacting in a dynamic process.

The brain is mainly composed of three components: the **cerebrum**, which is the largest part of the brain and controls higher functions, such as vision, hearing, and tasting; the **cerebellum**, which is the entity responsible for coordinating muscle movements and the general posture of the human body, including its balance; and the third part is called the **brainstem**, which connects the two previous parts and control many other tasks, including sneezing, coughing, and digesting.

The brain performs complex operations thanks to its different parts. Logically, the anatomy of the human brain is composed of many regions, so each region works based on a specific algorithm. Although each part of the brain works using its own algorithm, surprisingly, the human brain uses essentially the same algorithm to understand many different input modalities. This hypothesis is called the **one learning algorithm** hypothesis. Many studies done by *Roe et al.* in 1992 proved it, especially ferret experiments, in which the input for vision was plugged into auditory part of the ferret's brain, and the auditory cortex learned how to see.

The following diagram describes the relationship between **Artificial Intelligence (AI)**, **Machine Learning (ML)**, and **Deep Learning (DL)**:

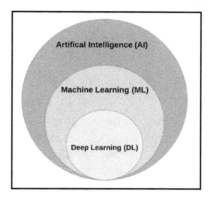

Biologically, the human brain is composed of billions of small organs called neurons. Neurons are units that process and transfer information through electrical and chemical signals. These nerve cells are mainly composed of:

- Dendrites
- Axons
- Synapses
- Cell body
- Nucleus

The following diagram illustrates the different components of a biological neuron:

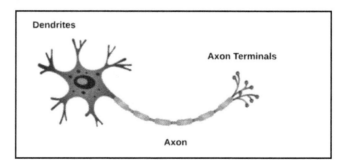

The analogical representation of a biological neuron is called a **perceptron**. The perceptron can be broken down into:

- Inputs
- Weights
- Net input function
- Activation function
- Output

The analogy between a perceptron and a human neuron is not totally correct. It is used just to give a glimpse into how a perceptron works. The human mind is far more complicated than artificial neural networks. There are a few similarities but a direct comparison between the mind and neural networks is not appropriate.

Implementing neural networks in Python

Classic computer programs are great when it comes to compute operations based on a sequence of instructions and arithmetic, but they face difficulties and challenges in many other cases; for example, handwriting-recognition. As a warm up, let's build a handwritten digit recognizer to take the opportunity to install the Python libraries needed in the next sections and learn how to build and implement our first neural network in Python. To train the model, we need to feed it with data. In our implementation, we are going to use the MNIST dataset:

First, let's install the `keras` library using the `pip install` command, as shown here:

```
# pip install keras
```

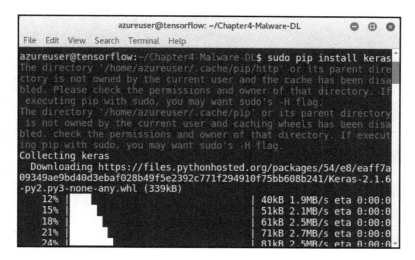

Then, install TensorFlow (`tensorflow`) using the following command:

```
# pip install tensorflow
```

And finally, install `np_utils`:

```
# pip install np_utils
```

```
azureuser@tensorflow: ~/Chapter4-Malware-DL
File  Edit  View  Search  Terminal  Help
azureuser@tensorflow:~/Chapter4-Malware-DL$ pip install np_utils
Collecting np_utils
  Downloading https://files.pythonhosted.org/packages/e7/9f/41532002ac86d2679abd68f642ae6392a63a7ccaf7
99fcb5870b03e72a80/np_utils-0.5.5.0.tar.gz (59kB)
    100% |                              | 61kB 2.2MB/s
Collecting numpy>=1.0 (from np_utils)
  Downloading https://files.pythonhosted.org/packages/76/4d/418dda252cf92bad00ab82d6b2a856e7843b47a5c2
f084aed34b14b67d64/numpy-1.14.2-cp27-cp27mu-manylinux1_x86_64.whl (12.1MB)
    100% |                              | 12.1MB 109kB/s
Collecting future>=0.16 (from np_utils)
  Downloading https://files.pythonhosted.org/packages/00/2b/8d082ddfed935f3608cc61140df6dcbf0edea1bc3a
b52fb6c29ae3e81e85/future-0.16.0.tar.gz (824kB)
    100% |                              | 829kB 1.6MB/s
Building wheels for collected packages: np-utils, future
  Running setup.py bdist_wheel for np-utils ... done
  Stored in directory: /home/azureuser/.cache/pip/wheels/45/57/c8/374ecee74d3b7cc32f026e5b473cdea11164
2d97f211478b6c
  Running setup.py bdist_wheel for future ... done
```

Open the Python command-line interface and import the following modules using the import commands as shown:

- The `mnist` dataset
- The `Sequential` model
- The `Dense` and `Dropout` layers
- The `np_utils` module

```
>>> from keras.models import Sequential
>>> from keras.layers import Dense
>>> from keras.layers import Dropout
>>> from keras.utils import np_utils
```

The following diagram illustrates the preceding code:

```
                        azureuser@tensorflow: ~/Chapter4-Malware-DL
File  Edit  View  Search  Terminal  Help
azureuser@tensorflow:~/Chapter4-Malware-DL$ python
Python 2.7.12 (default, Dec  4 2017, 14:50:18)
[GCC 5.4.0 20160609] on linux2
Type "help", "copyright", "credits" or "license" for more information.
>>> import numpy
>>> from keras.datasets import mnist
Using TensorFlow backend.
/usr/local/lib/python2.7/dist-packages/h5py/__init__.py:36: FutureWarning: Conversion of the second
argument of issubdtype from `float` to `np.floating` is deprecated. In future, it will be treated as
 `np.float64 == np.dtype(float).type`.
  from ._conv import register_converters as _register_converters
>>> from keras.models import Sequential
>>> from keras.layers import Dense
>>> from keras.layers import Dropout
>>> from keras.utils import np_utils
>>>
```

Seed is used because we want repeatable results. `numpy.random.seed(seed)` is used to seed the generator:

```
>>> seed = 7
>>> numpy.random.seed(seed)
>>> (X_train, y_train), (X_test, y_test) = mnist.load_data()
```

Download data from `https://s3.amazonaws.com/img-datasets/mnist.pkl.gz`:

```
>>> num_pixels = X_train.shape[1] * X_train.shape[2]
>>> X_train = X_train.reshape(X_train.shape[0],
num_pixels).astype('float32')
>>> X_test = X_test.reshape(X_test.shape[0], num_pixels).astype('float32')
>>> X_train = X_train / 255
>>> X_test = X_test / 255

>>> y_train = np_utils.to_categorical(y_train)
>>> y_test = np_utils.to_categorical(y_test)
>>> num_classes = y_test.shape[1]
>>> model = Sequential()
>>>model.add(Dense(num_pixels, input_dim=num_pixels, activation='relu'))
>>>model.add(Dense(num_classes,activation='softmax'))
>>>model.compile(loss='categorical_crossentropy', optimizer='adam',
metrics=['accuracy'])
```

Here, `.astype()` is used to convert the variables and `.reshape()` is used to give the array a new shape without changing the data:

```
azureuser@tensorflow: ~/Chapter4-Malware-DL
File  Edit  View  Search  Terminal  Help
8s - loss: 0.0526 - acc: 0.9850 - val_loss: 0.0648 - val_acc: 0.9808
Epoch 5/10
7s - loss: 0.0381 - acc: 0.9888 - val_loss: 0.0635 - val_acc: 0.9789
Epoch 6/10
8s - loss: 0.0270 - acc: 0.9927 - val_loss: 0.0619 - val_acc: 0.9789
Epoch 7/10
7s - loss: 0.0216 - acc: 0.9945 - val_loss: 0.0591 - val_acc: 0.9816
Epoch 8/10
8s - loss: 0.0148 - acc: 0.9967 - val_loss: 0.0577 - val_acc: 0.9812
Epoch 9/10
7s - loss: 0.0113 - acc: 0.9976 - val_loss: 0.0644 - val_acc: 0.9796
Epoch 10/10
8s - loss: 0.0089 - acc: 0.9981 - val_loss: 0.0648 - val_acc: 0.9800
<keras.callbacks.History object at 0x7f6ba92363d0>
>>> scores = model.evaluate(X_test, y_test, verbose=0)
>>> print("Baseline Error: %.2f%%" % (100-scores[1]*100))
Baseline Error: 2.00%
>>>
```

The accuracy of our handwritten digit classifier is 99.8%, which is an amazing result. Now we have learned how to build our first neural network program, it is time to leverage our skills and get hands-on experience in how to build malware classifiers using artificial neural networks, especially DL networks.

Deep learning model using PE headers

With the concepts we've learned, we are going to build a malware detector with artificial neural networks. Let's begin by identifying our dataset. By now, you are familiar with the steps required to build a machine learning models. For this model, we are going to use the **Portable Executable** (**PE**) files as feeding data. As you noticed in the previous chapter, we installed a Python library called `pefile`. It is time to use it in this model. Once we install `pefile` with the Python package installation manager PIP, we can start using `pefile` to extract information from any PE file. In order to gather information from a PE file, import the `os` and `pefile` libraries. The `os` library allows you to interface with the underlying operating system that Python is running on.

As a demonstration, we are going to download a malware PE file delivered by Palo Alto networks for experimental purposes. Download it with the `wget` command as follows:

```
# wget https://wildfire.paloaltonetworks.com/publicapi/test/pe
```

Once the PE file is installed, open the Python environment and import the required libraries, as shown here:

```
>>> import os
>>> import pefile
```

Load the file using the following command:

```
>>> PEfile = pefile.PE("pe", fast_load=True)
```

Now we are able to extract PE_HEADER_OPTIONAL information from the PE file, including MajorLinkerVersion, MajorLinkerVersion, SizeOfImage, and DllCharacteristics. You can find the full list by checking the Microsoft documentation:

```cpp
typedef struct _IMAGE_OPTIONAL_HEADER {
    WORD                 Magic;
    BYTE                 MajorLinkerVersion;
    BYTE                 MinorLinkerVersion;
    DWORD                SizeOfCode;
    DWORD                SizeOfInitializedData;
    DWORD                SizeOfUninitializedData;
    DWORD                AddressOfEntryPoint;
    DWORD                BaseOfCode;
    DWORD                BaseOfData;
    DWORD                ImageBase;
    DWORD                SectionAlignment;
    DWORD                FileAlignment;
    WORD                 MajorOperatingSystemVersion;
    WORD                 MinorOperatingSystemVersion;
    WORD                 MajorImageVersion;
    WORD                 MinorImageVersion;
    WORD                 MajorSubsystemVersion;
    WORD                 MinorSubsystemVersion;
    DWORD                Win32VersionValue;
    DWORD                SizeOfImage;
    DWORD                SizeOfHeaders;
    DWORD                CheckSum;
    WORD                 Subsystem;
    WORD                 DllCharacteristics;
    DWORD                SizeOfStackReserve;
    DWORD                SizeOfStackCommit;
    DWORD                SizeOfHeapReserve;
    DWORD                SizeOfHeapCommit;
    DWORD                LoaderFlags;
    DWORD                NumberOfRvaAndSizes;
    IMAGE_DATA_DIRECTORY DataDirectory[IMAGE_NUMBEROF_DIRECTORY_ENTRIES];
} IMAGE_OPTIONAL_HEADER, *PIMAGE_OPTIONAL_HEADER;
```

In the following script, I have extracted information about:

- `LinkerVersion`
- `NumberOfSections`
- `ImageVersion`

```
                         azureuser@tensorflow: ~/Chapter4-Malware-DL

File  Edit  View  Search  Terminal  Help
>>> import os
>>> import pefile
>>> LinkerVersion = PEfile.OPTIONAL_HEADER.MajorLinkerVersion
>>> print (LinkerVersion)
10
>>> NumberOfSections = PEfile.FILE_HEADER.NumberOfSections
>>> print (NumberOfSections)
4
>>> ImageVersion = PEfile.OPTIONAL_HEADER.MajorImageVersion
>>> print (ImageVersion)
5731
>>>
```

We know that training the model is a high-consumption task when it comes to computing. Thus, processing and feeding the model with all the header information is not a wise decision. So, we need to feature engineer them. Selecting the good features is a skill needed in every data science mission. A research study called *Selecting Features to Classify Malware* by Karthik Raman from the **Product Security Incident Response Team (PSIRT)**, Adobe Systems, made a proposal to solve that issue by suggesting the most important PE headers that we need to select; they are the following:

- `DebugSize`
- `DebugRVA`
- `ImageVersion`
- `OperatingSystemVersion`
- `SizeOfStackReserve`
- `LinkerVersion`

- DllCharacteristics
- IatRVA
- ExportSize
- ExportRVA
- ExportNameLen
- ResourceSize
- ExportFunctionsCount

To extract them, you can use the imported PEfile module like we did previously:

```
DebugSize = PEfile.OPTIONAL_HEADER.DATA_DIRECTORY[6].Size
print (DebugSize)
DebugRVA = PEfile.OPTIONAL_HEADER.DATA_DIRECTORY[6].VirtualAddress
print (DebugRVA)
 ImageVersion = PEfile.OPTIONAL_HEADER.MajorImageVersion
 print (ImageVersion)
OSVersion = PEfile.OPTIONAL_HEADER.MajorOperatingSystemVersion
print (OSVersion)
ExportRVA = PEfile.OPTIONAL_HEADER.DATA_DIRECTORY[0].VirtualAddress
 print (ExportRVA)
ExportSize = PEfile.OPTIONAL_HEADER.DATA_DIRECTORY[0].Size
print (ExportSize)
IATRVA = PEfile.OPTIONAL_HEADER.DATA_DIRECTORY[12].VirtualAddress
 print (IATRVA)
ResSize = PEfile.OPTIONAL_HEADER.DATA_DIRECTORY[2].Size
 print (ResSize)
LinkerVersion = PEfile.OPTIONAL_HEADER.MajorLinkerVersion
 print (LinkerVersion)
NumberOfSections = PEfile.FILE_HEADER.NumberOfSections
 print (NumberOfSections)
StackReserveSize = PEfile.OPTIONAL_HEADER.SizeOfStackReserve
 print (StackReserveSize)
Dll = PEfile.OPTIONAL_HEADER.DllCharacteristics
print (Dll)
```

```
                        azureuser@tensorflow: ~/Chapter4-Malware-DL          ⊖ ⊡ ⊗

 File  Edit  View  Search  Terminal  Help

>>> DebugSize = PEfile.OPTIONAL_HEADER.DATA_DIRECTORY[6].Size
>>> print (DebugSize)
0
>>> DebugRVA = PEfile.OPTIONAL_HEADER.DATA_DIRECTORY[6].VirtualAddress
>>> print (DebugRVA)
0
>>> ImageVersion = PEfile.OPTIONAL_HEADER.MajorImageVersion
>>> print (ImageVersion)
5731
>>> OSVersion = PEfile.OPTIONAL_HEADER.MajorOperatingSystemVersion
>>> print (OSVersion)
5
>>> ExportRVA = PEfile.OPTIONAL_HEADER.DATA_DIRECTORY[0].VirtualAddress
>>> print (ExportRVA)
0
>>> ExportSize = PEfile.OPTIONAL_HEADER.DATA_DIRECTORY[0].Size
>>> print (ExportSize)
0
>>> IATRVA = PEfile.OPTIONAL_HEADER.DATA_DIRECTORY[12].VirtualAddress
>>> print (IATRVA)
40960
>>> ResSize = PEfile.OPTIONAL_HEADER.DATA_DIRECTORY[2].Size
>>> print (ResSize)
0
>>> LinkerVersion = PEfile.OPTIONAL_HEADER.MajorLinkerVersion
>>> print (LinkerVersion)
10
>>> NumberOfSections = PEfile.FILE_HEADER.NumberOfSections
>>> print (NumberOfSections)
```

To train the model, there are many publicly available sources. You can download different types of file (clean and malicious) from a large list of organizations and educational institutions, such as:

- **ViruSign**: http://www.virusign.com/
- **MalShare**: http://malshare.com/
- **Malware DB**: http://ytisf.github.io/theZoo/
- **Endgame Malware BEnchmark for Research (EMBER)**: One of the largest datasets, this contains 1.1 million SHA256 hashes from PE files that were scanned sometime in 2017. I highly recommend you download it and try to build your models using it. You can download it from https://pubdata.endgame.com/ember/ember_dataset.tar.bz2 (1.6 GB, expands to 9.2 GB):

Your dataset should contain two categories of PE files: **clean** and **malicious files**. We need at least 10,000 files to train the model. You will have to start extracting header information using the previous scripts. You can automate the task by developing an automation script by yourself. Feel free to use any programming language. The best way is to export the selected features of all the files to CSV files so we can use what we learned in the previous chapters, and so we can later load them using pandas:

```
Malware   = pd.read_csv("Malware.csv")
Clean_Files = pd.read_csv("Clean_Files.csv")
```

After preparing the features, we need to merge the two types of data into one. For example, we can use pd.concat to merge the two files. To train the model, we need to import the required modules:

```
>>> import numpy as np
>>> from sklearn.model_selection import train_test_split
>>> from sklearn.metrics import confusion_matrix
>>> from sklearn.neural_network import MLPClassifier
>>> from sklearn.preprocessing import StandardScaler
```

For data preparation:

```
y = dataset['Clean_Files']
X = dataset.drop('Clean_Files',axis = 1)
X = np.asarray(X)
y = np.asarray(y)
```

This line is for splitting, as we did in the other models:

```
X_train,X_test,y_train,y_test = train_test_split(X,y,test_size =
0.3,random_state=0)
```

For better prediction, we can use `StandScaler()`; it is used for standardizing features by removing the mean and scaling to unit variance:

```
scaler = StandardScaler()
scaler.fit(X_train)
X_train = scaler.transform(X_train)
X_test = scaler.transform(X_test)
```

After preparing and feature engineering the data, we have to build the **Multi-Layer Perceptron (MLP)** network:

```
MLP = MLPClassifier(hidden_layer_sizes=(12,12,12,12,12,12))
```

Here, `12` is the number of layers and the number of features. Let's train the model and compute the predictions:

```
MLP.fit(X_train,y_train)
Predictions = MLP.predict(X_test)
```

To check the evaluation metrics, add the following line:

```
TN, FP, FN TP = confusion_matrix(y_test,predictions).ravel()
```

`ravel()` is used here to return a contiguous flattened array. It is equivalent to `reshape(-1, order=order)`:

```
print ("True Positive:" , TP)
print ("True Negative:" , TN)
print ("False Positive:" , FP)
print ("False Negative:" , FN)
```

Deep learning model with convolutional neural networks and malware visualization

The previous section was a real-world implementation of MLP networks for detecting malware. Now, we are going to explore other artificial network architectures and we are also going to learn how to use one of them to help malware analysts and information security professionals to detect and classify malicious code. Before diving into the technical details and the steps for the practical implementation of the DL method, it is essential to learn and discover the other different architectures of artificial neural networks. We discussed some of them briefly in Chapter 1, *Introduction to Machine Learning in Pentesting*. The major artificial neural networks are discussed now.

Convolutional Neural Networks (CNNs)

Convolutional Neural Networks (CNNs) are a deep learning approach to tackle the image classification problem, or what we call computer vision problems, because classic computer programs face many challenges and difficulties to identify objects for many reasons, including lighting, viewpoint, deformation, and segmentation. This technique is inspired by how the eye works, especially the visual cortex function algorithm in animals. In CNN are arranged in three-dimensional structures with width, height, and depth as characteristics. In the case of images, the height is the image height, the width is the image width, and the depth is RGB channels. To build a CNN, we need three main types of layer:

- **Convolutional layer**: A convolutional operation refers to extracting features from the input image and multiplying the values in the filter with the original pixel values
- **Pooling layer**: The pooling operation reduces the dimensionality of each feature map
- **Fully-connected layer**: The fully-connected layer is a classic multi-layer perceptrons with a softmax activation function in the output layer

To implement a CNN with Python, you can use the following Python script:

```python
import numpy
from keras.datasets import mnist
from keras.models import Sequential
from keras.layers import Dense
from keras.layers import Dropout
from keras.layers import Flatten
from keras.layers.convolutional import Conv2D
from keras.layers.convolutional import MaxPooling2D
from keras.utils import np_utils
from keras import backend
backend.set_image_dim_ordering('th')

model = Sequential()
model.add(Conv2D(32, (5, 5), input_shape=(1, 28, 28), activation='relu'))
model.add(MaxPooling2D(pool_size=(2, 2)))
model.add(Dropout(0.2))
model.add(Flatten())
model.add(Dense(128, activation='relu'))
model.add(Dense(num_classes, activation='softmax'))
model.compile(loss='categorical_crossentropy', optimizer='adam',
metrics=['accuracy'])
```

Recurrent Neural Networks (RNNs)

Recurrent Neural Networks (**RNNs**) are artificial neural networks where we can make use of sequential information, such as sentences. In other words, RNNs perform the same task for every element of a sequence, with the output depending on the previous computations. RNNs are widely used in language modeling and text generation (machine translation, speech recognition, and many other applications). RNNs do not remember things for a long time.

Long Short Term Memory networks

Long Short Term Memory (**LSTM**) solves the short memory issue in recurrent neural networks by building a memory block. This block sometimes is called a **memory cell**.

Hopfield networks

Hopfield networks were developed by John Hopfield in 1982. The main goal of Hopfield networks is auto-association and optimization. We have two categories of Hopfield network: **discrete** and **continuous**.

Boltzmann machine networks

Boltzmann machine networks use recurrent structures and they use only locally available information. They were developed by Geoffrey Hinton and Terry Sejnowski in 1985. Also, the goal of a Boltzmann machine is optimizing the solutions.

Malware detection with CNNs

For this new model, we are going to discover how to build a malware classifier with CNNs. But I bet you are wondering how we can do that while CNNs are taking images as inputs. The answer is really simple, the trick here is converting malware into an image. Is this possible? Yes, it is. Malware visualization is one of many research topics during the past few years. One of the proposed solutions has came from a research study called *Malware Images: Visualization and Automatic Classification* by *Lakshmanan Nataraj* from the Vision Research Lab, University of California, Santa Barbara.

The following diagram details how to convert malware into an image:

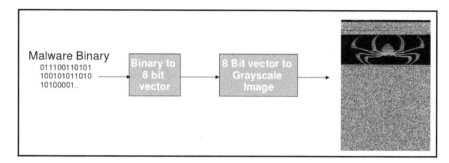

The following is an image of the **Alueron.gen!J** malware:

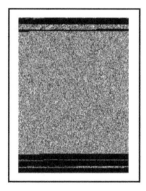

This technique also gives us the ability to visualize malware sections in a detailed way:

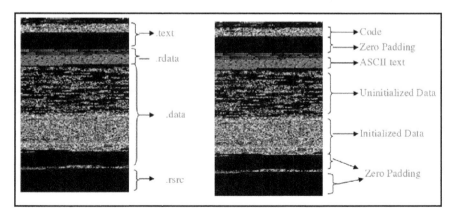

By solving the issue of how to feed malware machine learning classifiers that use CNNs by images, information security professionals can use the power of CNNs to train models. One of the malware datasets most often used to feed CNNs is the **Malimg dataset**. This malware dataset contains 9,339 malware samples from 25 different malware families. You can download it from Kaggle (a platform for predictive modeling and analytics competitions) by visiting this link: `https://www.kaggle.com/afagarap/malimg-dataset/data`.

These are the malware families:

- Allaple.L
- Allaple.A
- Yuner.A
- Lolyda.AA 1
- Lolyda.AA 2
- Lolyda.AA 3
- C2Lop.P
- C2Lop.gen!G
- Instant access
- Swizzor.gen!I
- Swizzor.gen!E
- VB.AT
- Fakerean
- Alueron.gen!J
- Malex.gen!J
- Lolyda.AT
- Adialer.C
- Wintrim.BX
- Dialplatform.B
- Dontovo.A
- Obfuscator.AD
- Agent.FYI
- Autorun.K
- Rbot!gen
- Skintrim.N

After converting malware into grayscale images, you can get the following malware representation so you can use them later to feed the machine learning model:

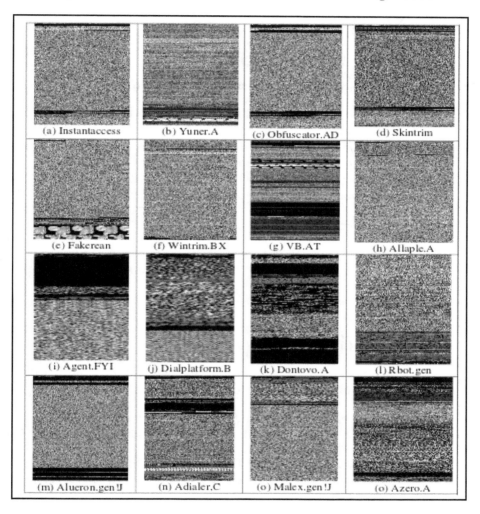

(a) Instantaccess   (b) Yuner.A   (c) Obfuscator.AD   (d) Skintrim

(e) Fakerean   (f) Wintrim.B X   (g) VB.AT   (h) Allaple.A

(i) Agent.FYI   (j) Dialplatform.B   (k) Dontovo.A   (l) Rbot.gen

(m) Alueron.gen !J   (n) Adialer.C   (o) Malex.gen !J   (o) Azero.A

The conversion of each malware to a grayscale image can be done using the following Python script:

```
import os
import scipy
import array
 filename = '<Malware_File_Name_Here>';
 f = open(filename,'rb');
```

```
      ln = os.path.getsize(filename);
    width = 256;
     rem = ln%width;
     a = array.array("B");
     a.fromfile(f,ln-rem);
     f.close();
     g = numpy.reshape(a, (len(a)/width,width));
     g = numpy.uint8(g);
     scipy.misc.imsave('<Malware_File_Name_Here>.png',g);
```

For feature selection, you can extract or use any image characteristics, such as the texture pattern, frequencies in image, intensity, or color features, using different techniques such as **Euclidean distance**, or mean and standard deviation, to generate later feature vectors. In our case, we can use algorithms such as a color layout descriptor, homogeneous texture descriptor, or **global image descriptors** (**GIST**). Let's suppose that we selected the GIST; pyleargist is a great Python library to compute it. To install it, use PIP as usual:

```
# pip install pyleargist==1.0.1
```

As a use case, to compute a GIST, you can use the following Python script:

```
import Image
Import leargist
  image = Image.open('<Image_Name_Here>.png');
  New_im = image.resize((64,64));
des = leargist.color_gist(New_im);
Feature_Vector = des[0:320];
```

Here, 320 refers to the first 320 values while we are using grayscale images. Don't forget to save them as *NumPy arrays* to use them later to train the model.

After getting the feature vectors, we can train many different models, including SVM, k-means, and artificial neural networks. One of the useful algorithms is that of the CNN.

Once the feature selection and engineering is done, we can build a CNN. For our model, for example, we will build a convolutional network with two convolutional layers, with *32 * 32* inputs. To build the model using Python libraries, we can implement it with the previously installed TensorFlow and utils libraries.

So the overall CNN architecture will be as in the following diagram:

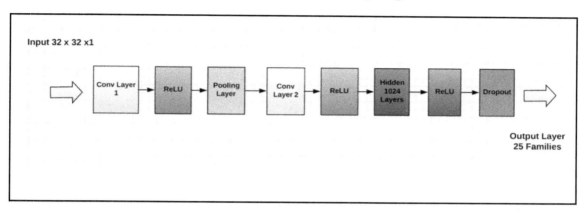

This CNN architecture is not the only proposal to build the model, but at the moment we are going to use it for the implementation.

To build the model and CNN in general, I highly recommend Keras. The required imports are the following:

```
import keras
  from keras.models import Sequential,Input,Model
  from keras.layers import Dense, Dropout, Flatten
  from keras.layers import Conv2D, MaxPooling2D
  from keras.layers.normalization import BatchNormalization
  from keras.layers.advanced_activations import LeakyReLU
```

As we discussed before, the grayscale image has pixel values that range from 0 to 255, and we need to feed the net with *32 * 32 * 1* dimension images as a result:

```
train_X = train_X.reshape(-1, 32,32, 1)
test_X = test_X.reshape(-1, 32,32, 1)
```

We will train our network with these parameters:

```
batch_size = 64
epochs = 20
num_classes = 25
```

To build the architecture, with regards to its format, use the following:

```
Malware_Model = Sequential()
Malware_Model.add(Conv2D(32,
kernel_size=(3,3),activation='linear',input_shape=(32,32,1),padding='same')
)
```

```
Malware_Model.add(LeakyReLU(alpha=0.1))
Malware_model.add(MaxPooling2D(pool_size=(2, 2),padding='same'))
Malware_Model.add(Conv2D(64, (3, 3), activation='linear',padding='same'))
Malware_Model.add(LeakyReLU(alpha=0.1))
Malware_Model.add(Dense(1024, activation='linear'))
Malware_Model.add(LeakyReLU(alpha=0.1))
Malware_Model.add(Dropout(0.4))
Malware_Model.add(Dense(num_classes, activation='softmax'))
```

To compile the model, use the following:

```
Malware_Model.compile(loss=keras.losses.categorical_crossentropy,
optimizer=keras.optimizers.Adam(),metrics=['accuracy'])
```

Fit and train the model:

```
Malware_Model.fit(train_X, train_label,
batch_size=batch_size,epochs=epochs,verbose=1,validation_data=(valid_X,
valid_label))
```

As you noticed, we are respecting the flow of training a neural network that was discussed in previous chapters. To evaluate the model, use the following code:

```
Malware_Model.evaluate(test_X, test_Y_one_hot, verbose=0)
print('The accuracy of the Test is:', test_eval[1])
```

Promises and challenges in applying deep learning to malware detection

Many different deep network architectures were proposed by machine learning practitioners and malware analysts to detect both known and unknown malware; some of the proposed architectures include restricted Boltzmann machines and hybrid methods. You can check some of them in the *Further reading* section. Novel approaches to detect malware and malicious software show many promising results. However, there are many challenges that malware analysts face when it comes to detecting malware using deep learning networks, especially when analyzing PE files because to analyze a PE file, we take each byte as an input unit, so we deal with classifying sequences with millions of steps, in addition to the need of keeping complicated spatial correlation across functions due to function calls and jump commands.

Summary

Malware is a nightmare for every modern organization. Attackers and cyber criminals are always coming up with new malicious software to attack their targets. Security vendors are doing their best to defend against malware attacks but, unfortunately, with millions of malwares discovered monthly, they cannot achieve that. Thus, novel approaches are needed, which are exactly what we looked at in this and the previous chapter. We discovered how to build malware detectors using different machine learning algorithms, especially using the power of deep learning techniques. In the next chapter, we will learn how to detect botnets by building and developing robust intelligent systems.

Questions

1. What is the difference between MLP networks and deep learning networks?
2. Why DL recently is taking off?
3. Why do we need to iterate multiple times through different models?
4. What type of DL needed to translate English to French language?
5. Why malware visualization is a good method to classify malware?
6. What is the role of an activation function?
7. Can you mention three DL architectures?

Further reading

- **Blog posts**:
    - Keras Tutorial: Deep Learning in Python (https://www.datacamp.com/community/tutorials/deep-learning-python)
    - Develop Your First Neural Network in Python With Keras Step-By-Step (https://machinelearningmastery.com/tutorial-first-neural-network-python-keras/)
    - THE MNIST Database of handwritten digits (http://yann.lecun.com/exdb/mnist/)

- **Papers and presentations**:
    - High dimensional visualization of malware families (`https://www.rsaconference.com/writable/presentations/file_upload/tta-f04-high-dimensional-visualization-of-malware-families.pdf`)
    - A Hybrid Malicious Code Detection Method based on Deep Learning (`http://www.covert.io/research-papers/deep-learning-security/A%20Hybrid%20Malicious%20Code%20Detection%20Method%20based%20on%20Deep%20Learning.pdf`)
    - A Multi-task Learning Model for Malware Classification with Useful File Access Pattern from API Call Sequence (`http://www.covert.io/research-papers/deep-learning-security/A%20Multi-task%20Learning%20Model%20for%20Malware%20Classification%20with%20Useful%20File%20Access%20Pattern%20from%20API%20Call%20Sequence.pdf`)
    - Combining Restricted Boltzmann Machine and One Side Perceptron for Malware Detection (`http://www.covert.io/research-papers/deep-learning-security/Combining%20Restricted%20Boltzmann%20Machine%20and%20One%20Side%20Perceptron%20for%20Malware%20Detection.pdf`)
    - Convolutional Neural Networks for Malware Classification- Thesis (`http://www.covert.io/research-papers/deep-learning-security/Convolutional%20Neural%20Networks%20for%20Malware%20Classification.pdf`)
    - Deep Learning for Classification of Malware System Call Sequences (`http://www.covert.io/research-papers/deep-learning-security/Deep%20Learning%20for%20Classification%20of%20Malware%20System%20Call%20Sequences.pdf`)

- Deep Neural Network Based Malware Detection using Two Dimensional Binary Program Features (`http://www.covert.io/research-papers/deep-learning-security/Deep%20Neural%20Network%20Based%20Malware%20Detection%20Using%20Two%20Dimensional%20Binary%20Program%20Features.pdf`)

- DL4MD: A Deep Learning Framework for Intelligent Malware Detection (`http://www.covert.io/research-papers/deep-learning-security/DL4MD-%20A%20Deep%20Learning%20Framework%20for%20Intelligent%20Malware%20Detection.pdf`)

- Droid-Sec: Deep Learning in Android Malware Detection (`http://www.covert.io/research-papers/deep-learning-security/DroidSec%20-%20Deep%20Learning%20in%20Android%20Malware%20Detection.pdf`)

- HADM: Hybrid Analysis for Detection of Malware (`http://www.covert.io/research-papers/deep-learning-security/HADM-%20Hybrid%20Analysis%20for%20Detection%20of%20Malware.pdf`)

- Malware Classification with Recurrent Networks (`http://www.covert.io/research-papers/deep-learning-security/Malware%20Classification%20with%20Recurrent%20Networks.pdf`)

Botnet Detection with Machine Learning

5

Nowadays, connected devices play an important role in modern life. From smart home appliances, computers, coffee machines, and cameras, to connected cars, this huge shift in our lifestyles has made our lives easier. Unfortunately, these exposed devices could be attacked and accessed by attackers and cyber criminals who could use them later to enable larger-scale attacks. Security vendors provide many solutions and products to defend against botnets, but in this chapter, as we did in previous chapters, we are going to learn how to build novel botnet detection systems with Python and machine learning techniques.

In this chapter, we will see:

- An overview of botnets
- How to build a botnet detector with different machine learning algorithms
- How to build a Twitter bot detector

Technical requirements

You will find all the code discussed, in addition to some other useful scripts, in the following repository: `https://github.com/PacktPublishing/Mastering-Machine-Learning-for-Penetration-Testing/tree/master/Chapter5`.

Botnet overview

Botnet is a combination of the two terms **bot** and **net**. The bot part represents the fact that this malware automates things and tasks like a robot. The second part refers to a network, in other words, a network of compromised devices. So, by definition, a botnet is a form of malware that attacks computers on the internet and controls them with command and control servers to perform a wide variety of automated tasks, including sending spam emails and performing **Distributed Denial of Service** (**DDoS**) attacks. Attacked machines join an immense network of compromised machines. One of the most notable botnets in previous years was the *Mirai botnet*. Mirai means *the future* in Japanese. This botnet hit millions of online devices, especially **Internet of Things** (**IoT**) appliances, by scanning and identifying vulnerable machines, taking advantage of the fact that most of them are accessed using default login credentials. Some of the tasks performed by botnets are:

- Advertising fraud and sending spam emails
- Cryptocurrency mining
- Stealing personal data and sensitive information
- Performing DDoS attacks
- Performing brute force attacks

The following diagram describes the different actors of a botnet ecosystem:

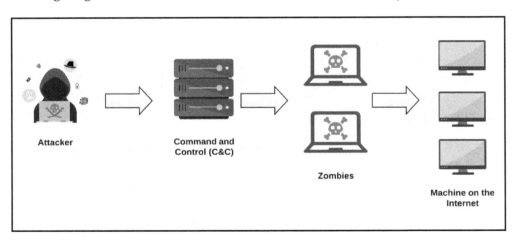

Hacking is a methodological task. Criminals and cyber attackers usually use the same defined steps. As you are penetration testers and information security professionals, you are aware of the hacking phases, which are information gathering, or what we call reconnaissance; scanning; gaining access; maintaining access; and finally clearing tracks. Thus, botnets usually respect some defined steps. Botnets work based on four different phases:

- **Infection**: In this phase, the attackers infect the targeted machines by sending the malware.
- **Connection**: In this phase, the botnet initiates an internet connection with the control and command server to receive the commands and automated tasks.
- **Control**: In this phase, the attack occurs, for example, sending spam emails.
- **Multiplication**: In this phase, the botnet will try to compromise more machine to join them in the network and become what we call **zombies**:

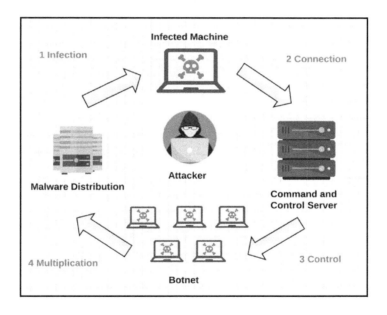

Building a botnet detector model with multiple machine learning techniques

In this section, we are going to learn how to build different botnet detection systems with many machine learning algorithms. As a start to a first practical lab, let's start by building a machine learning-based botnet detector using different classifiers. By now, I hope you have acquired a clear understanding about the major steps of building machine learning systems. So, I believe that you already know that, as a first step, we need to look for a dataset. Many educational institutions and organizations are given a set of collected datasets from internal laboratories. One of the most well known botnet datasets is called the **CTU-13** dataset. It is a labeled dataset with botnet, normal, and background traffic delivered by CTU University, Czech Republic. During their work, they tried to capture real botnet traffic mixed with normal traffic and background traffic. To download the dataset and check out more information about it, you can visit the following link: `https://mcfp.weebly.com/the-ctu-13-dataset-a-labeled-dataset-with-botnet-normal-and-background-traffic.html`.

The dataset is bidirectional NetFlow files. But what are bidirectional NetFlow files? Netflow is an internet protocol developed by Cisco. The goal of this protocol is to collect IP traffic information and monitor network traffic in order to have a clearer view about the network traffic flow. The main components of a NetFlow architecture are a **NetFlow Exporter**, a **Netflow collector**, and a **Flow Storage**. The following diagram illustrates the different components of a NetFlow infrastructure:

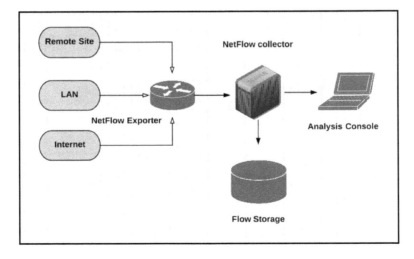

When it comes to NetFlow generally, when host A sends an information to **host B** and from **host B** to **host A** as a reply, the operation is named unidirectional NetFlow. The sending and the reply are considered different operations. In bidirectional NetFlow, we consider the flows from **host A** and **host B** as one flow. Let's download the dataset by using the following command:

```
$ wget --no-check-certificate
https://mcfp.felk.cvut.cz/publicDatasets/CTU-13-Dataset/CTU-13-Dataset.tar.
bz2
```

Extract the downloaded `tar.bz2` file by using the following command:

```
# tar xvjf  CTU-13-Dataset.tar.bz2
```

The file contains all the datasets, with the different scenarios. For the demonstration, we are going to use dataset 8 (scenario 8). You can select any scenario or you can use your own collected data, or any other .binetflow files delivered by other institutions:

Load the data using pandas as usual:

```
>>> import pandas as pd
>>> data = pd.read_csv("capture20110816-3.binetflow")
>>> data['Label'] = data.Label.str.contains("Botnet")
```

Exploring the data is essential in any data-centric project. For example, you can start by checking the names of the features or the columns:

```
>> data.columns
```

The command results in the columns of the dataset: StartTime, Dur, Proto, SrcAddr, Sport, Dir, DstAddr, Dport, State, sTos, dTos, TotPkts, TotBytes, SrcBytes, and Label. The columns represent the features used in the dataset; for example, Dur represents duration, Sport represent the source port, and so on. You can find the full list of features in the chapter's GitHub repository.

Before training the model, we need to build some scripts to prepare the data. This time, we are going to build a separate Python script to prepare data, and later we can just import it into the main script.

I will call the first script DataPreparation.py. There are many proposals done to help extract the features and prepare data to build botnet detectors using machine learning. In our case, I customized two new scripts inspired by the data loading scripts built by *NagabhushanS*:

```
from __future__ import division
import os, sys
import threading
```

After importing the required Python packages, we created a class called `Prepare` to select training and testing data:

```
class Prepare(threading.Thread):
def __init__(self, X, Y, XT, YT, accLabel=None):
    threading.Thread.__init__(self)
    self.X = X
    self.Y = Y
    self.XT=XT
    self.YT=YT
    self.accLabel= accLabel


def run(self):
    X = np.zeros(self.X.shape)
    Y = np.zeros(self.Y.shape)
    XT = np.zeros(self.XT.shape)
    YT = np.zeros(self.YT.shape)
    np.copyto(X, self.X)
    np.copyto(Y, self.Y)
    np.copyto(XT, self.XT)
    np.copyto(YT, self.YT)
    for i in range(9):
        X[:, i] = (X[:, i] - X[:, i].mean()) / (X[:, i].std())
    for i in range(9):
        XT[:, i] = (XT[:, i] - XT[:, i].mean()) / (XT[:, i].std())
```

The second script is called `LoadData.py`. You can find it on GitHub and use it directly in your projects to load data from `.binetflow` files and generate a `pickle` file.

Let's use what we developed previously to train the models. After building the data loader and preparing the machine learning algorithms that we are going to use, it is time to train and test the models.

First, load the data from the `pickle` file, which is why we need to import the `pickle` Python library. Don't forget to import the previous scripts using:

```
import LoadData
import DataPreparation
import pickle
file = open('flowdata.pickle', 'rb')
data = pickle.load(file)
```

Select the data sections:

```
Xdata = data[0]
Ydata =  data[1]
XdataT = data[2]
YdataT = data[3]
```

As machine learning classifiers, we are going to try many different algorithms so later we can select the best algorithm for our model. Import the required modules to use four machine learning algorithms from `sklearn`:

```
from sklearn.linear_model import *
from sklearn.tree import *
from sklearn.naive_bayes import *
from sklearn.neighbors import *
```

Prepare the data by using the previous module build. Don't forget to import `DataPreparation` by typing `import DataPreparation`:

```
>>> DataPreparation.Prepare(Xdata,Ydata,XdataT,YdataT)
```

Now, we can train the models; and to do that, we are going to train the model with different techniques so later we can select the most suitable machine learning technique for our project. The steps are like what we learned in previous projects: after preparing the data and selecting the features, define the machine learning algorithm, fit the model, and print out the score after defining its variable.

As machine learning classifiers, we are going to test many of them. Let's start with a decision tree:

- **Decision tree model**:

```
>>> clf = DecisionTreeClassifier()
>>> clf.fit(Xdata,Ydata)
>>> Prediction = clf.predict(XdataT)
>>> Score = clf.score(XdataT,YdataT)
>>> print ("The Score of the Decision Tree Classifier is",
Score * 100)
```

```
root@kali: /home/ghost/Chapter5/BotnetDetector
File  Edit  View  Search  Terminal  Help
>>> clf = DecisionTreeClassifier()
>>> clf.fit(Xdata,Ydata)
DecisionTreeClassifier(class_weight=None, criterion='gini', max_depth=None,
            max_features=None, max_leaf_nodes=None,
            min_impurity_decrease=0.0, min_impurity_split=None,
            min_samples_leaf=1, min_samples_split=2,
            min_weight_fraction_leaf=0.0, presort=False, random_state=None,
            splitter='best')
>>> Prediction = clf.predict(XdataT)
>>> Score = clf.score(XdataT,YdataT)
>>> print ("The Score of the Decision Tree Classifier is", Score * 100)
('The Score of the Decision Tree Classifier is', '99.91001799640073')
>>>
```

The score of the decision tree classifier is 99%

- **Logistic regression model**:

```
>>> clf = LogisticRegression(C=10000)
>>> clf.fit(Xdata,Ydata)
>>> Prediction = clf.predict(XdataT)
>>> Score = clf.score(XdataT,YdataT)
```

```
>>> print ("The Score of the Logistic Regression Classifier
is", Score * 100)
```

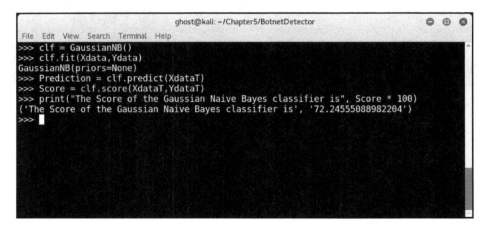

```
root@kali: /home/ghost/Chapter5/BotnetDetector
File  Edit  View  Search  Terminal  Help
>>> clf = LogisticRegression(C=10000)
>>> clf.fit(Xdata,Ydata)
LogisticRegression(C=10000, class_weight=None, dual=False, fit_intercept=True,
          intercept_scaling=1, max_iter=100, multi_class='ovr', n_jobs=1,
          penalty='l2', random_state=None, solver='liblinear', tol=0.0001,
          verbose=0, warm_start=False)
>>> Prediction = clf.predict(XdataT)
>>> Score = clf.score(XdataT,YdataT)
>>> print ("The Score of the Logistic Regression Classifier is", Score * 100)
('The Score of the Logistic Regression Classifier is', '96.67066586682664')
>>>
```

The score of the logistic regression classifier is 96%

- **Gaussian Naive Bayes model**:

```
>>> clf = GaussianNB()
>>> clf.fit(Xdata,Ydata)
>>> Prediction = clf.predict(XdataT)
>>> Score = clf.score(XdataT,YdataT)
>>> print("The Score of the Gaussian Naive Bayes classifier
is", Score * 100)
```

```
ghost@kali: ~/Chapter5/BotnetDetector
File  Edit  View  Search  Terminal  Help
>>> clf = GaussianNB()
>>> clf.fit(Xdata,Ydata)
GaussianNB(priors=None)
>>> Prediction = clf.predict(XdataT)
>>> Score = clf.score(XdataT,YdataT)
>>> print("The Score of the Gaussian Naive Bayes classifier is", Score * 100)
('The Score of the Gaussian Naive Bayes classifier is', '72.24555088982204')
>>>
```

The score of the Gaussian Naive Bayes classifier is 72%

- **k-Nearest Neighbors model**:

```
>>> clf = KNeighborsClassifier()
>>> clf.fit(Xdata,Ydata)
>>> Prediction = clf.predict(XdataT)
>>> Score = clf.score(XdataT,YdataT)
>>> print("The Score of the K-Nearest Neighbours classifier
is", Score * 100)
```

```
ghost@kali: ~/Chapter5/BotnetDetector

File  Edit  View  Search  Terminal  Help

>>> clf = KNeighborsClassifier()
>>> clf.fit(Xdata,Ydata)
KNeighborsClassifier(algorithm='auto', leaf_size=30, metric='minkowski',
          metric_params=None, n_jobs=1, n_neighbors=5, p=2,
          weights='uniform')
>>> Prediction = clf.predict(XdataT)
>>> Score = clf.score(XdataT,YdataT)
>>> print("The Score of the K-Nearest Neighbours classifier is", Score * 100)
('The Score of the K-Nearest Neighbours classifier is', '96.24075184963007')
>>>
```

The score of the k-Nearest Neighbors classifier is 96%

- **Neural network model**:

To build a Neural network Model use the following code:

```
>>> from keras.models import *
>>> from keras.layers import Dense, Activation
>>> from keras.optimizers import *


model = Sequential()
model.add(Dense(10, input_dim=9, activation="sigmoid"))
model.add(Dense(10, activation='sigmoid'))
model.add(Dense(1))
sgd = SGD(lr=0.01, decay=0.000001, momentum=0.9, nesterov=True)
model.compile(optimizer=sgd, loss='mse')
model.fit(Xdata, Ydata, nb_epoch=200, batch_size=100)
Score = model.evaluate(XdataT, YdataT, verbose=0)
Print("The Score of the Neural Network is", Score * 100  )
```

With this code, we imported the required Keras modules, we built the layers, we compiled the model with an SGD optimizer, we fit the model, and we printed out the score of the model.

How to build a Twitter bot detector

In the previous sections, we saw how to build a machine learning-based botnet detector. In this new project, we are going to deal with a different problem instead of defending against botnet malware. We are going to detect Twitter bots because they are also dangerous and can perform malicious actions. For the model, we are going to use the *NYU Tandon Spring 2017 Machine Learning Competition: Twitter Bot classification* dataset. You can download it from this link: `https://www.kaggle.com/c/twitter-bot-classification/data`. Import the required Python packages:

```
>>> import pandas as pd
>>> import numpy as np
>>> import seaborn
```

Let's load the data using pandas and highlight the bot and non-bot data:

```
>>> data = pd.read_csv('training_data_2_csv_UTF.csv')
>>> Bots = data[data.bot==1]
>> NonBots = data[data.bot==0]
```

Visualization with seaborn

In every project, I want to help you discover new data visualization Python libraries because, as you saw, data engineering and visualization are essential to every modern data-centric project. This time, I chose seaborn to visualize the data and explore it before starting the training phase. Seaborn is a Python library for making statistical visualizations. The following is an example of generating a plot with seaborn:

```
>>> data = np.random.multivariate_normal([0, 0], [[5, 2], [2, 2]],
size=2000)
>>> data = pd.DataFrame(data, columns=['x', 'y'])
>>> for col in 'xy':
... seaborn.kdeplot(data[col], shade=True)
```

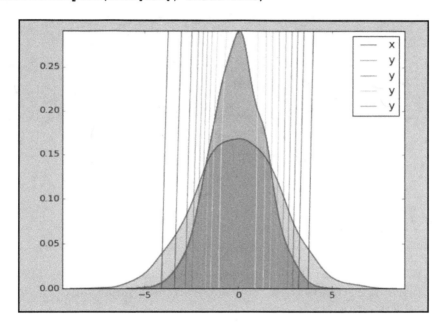

For example, in our case, if we want to identify the missing data:

```
matplotlib.pyplot.figure(figsize=(10,6))
  seaborn.heatmap(data.isnull(), yticklabels=False, cbar=False,
cmap='viridis')
  matplotlib.pyplot.tight_layout()
```

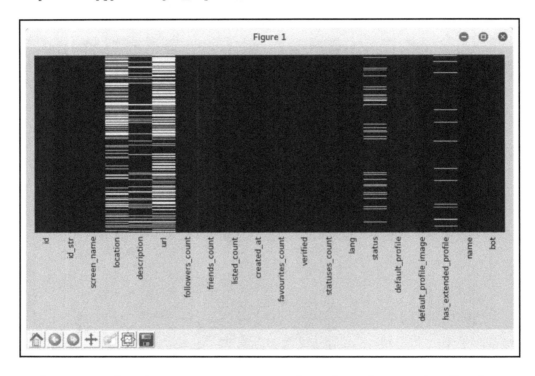

The previous two code snippets were some examples to learn how to visualize data. Visualization helps data scientists to explore and learn more about the data. Now, let's go back and continue building our model.

Identify the bag of words by selecting some bad words used by Twitter bots. The following is an example of bad words used by a bot. Of course, you can add more words:

```
bag_of_words_bot = r'bot|b0t|cannabis|tweet me|mishear|follow me|updates
every|gorilla|yes_ofc|forget' \
r'expos|kill|bbb|truthe|fake|anony|free|virus|funky|RNA|jargon' \
r'nerd|swag|jack|chick|prison|paper|pokem|xx|freak|ffd|dunia|clone|genie|bb
b' \
r'ffd|onlyman|emoji|joke|troll|droop|free|every|wow|cheese|yeah|bio|magic|w
izard|face'
```

- Now, it is time to identify training features:

```
data['screen_name_binary'] =
data.screen_name.str.contains(bag_of_words_bot, case=False, na=False)
data['name_binary'] = data.name.str.contains(bag_of_words_bot, case=False,
na=False)
data['description_binary'] =
data.description.str.contains(bag_of_words_bot, case=False, na=False)
data['status_binary'] = data.status.str.contains(bag_of_words_bot,
case=False, na=False)
```

- Feature extraction: Let's select features to use in our model:

```
data['listed_count_binary'] = (data.listed_count>20000)==False
 features = ['screen_name_binary', 'name_binary',
 'description_binary', 'status_binary', 'verified',
 'followers_count', 'friends_count', 'statuses_count',
 'listed_count_binary', 'bot']
```

- Now, train the model with a decision tree classifier:

```
from sklearn.tree import DecisionTreeClassifier
from sklearn.metrics import accuracy_score, roc_curve, auc
from sklearn.model_selection import train_test_split
```

- We import some previously discussed modules:

```
X = data[features].iloc[:,:-1]
y = data[features].iloc[:,-1]
```

- We define the classifier:

```
clf = DecisionTreeClassifier(criterion='entropy',
min_samples_leaf=50, min_samples_split=10)
```

- We split the classifier:

```
X_train, X_test, y_train, y_test = train_test_split(X, y,
test_size=0.3, random_state=101)
```

- We fit the model:

```
clf.fit(X_train, y_train)
y_pred_train = clf.predict(X_train)
y_pred_test = clf.predict(X_test)
```

- We print out the accuracy scores:

```
print("Training Accuracy: %.5f" %accuracy_score(y_train,
y_pred_train))
print("Test Accuracy: %.5f" %accuracy_score(y_test, y_pred_test))
```

Our model detects Twitter bots with an 88% detection rate, which is a good accuracy rate.

This technique is not the only possible way to detect botnets. Researchers have proposed many other models based on different machine learning algorithms, such as Linear SVM and decision trees. All these techniques have an accuracy of 90%. Most studies showed that feature engineering was a key contributor to improving machine learning models.

 To study a real-world case, check out a paper called *What we learn from learning - Understanding capabilities and limitations of machine learning in botnet attacks* (https://arxiv.org/pdf/1805.01333.pdf), conducted by David Santana, Shan Suthaharan, and Somya Mohanty.

Summary

This chapter was a lightweight guide to learning about botnet fundamentals and how to build a machine learning-based detector using different techniques. Also, we discussed how to identify Twitter bots. The next chapter will dive deep into anomalies and how to build many projects to identify anomalies using novel approaches.

Questions

As we do after every chapter, we are going to give you the opportunity to practice what you learned and evaluate your skills. This chapter's GitHub repository contains a link to a botnet traffic dataset in the Practice folder:

1. Download the dataset and load it with the pandas library
2. Select suitable features
3. Identify the training and testing sets, then export them into a pickle file
4. Load the pickle file
5. Import a support vector machine classifier and fit the model
6. Train the SVM model
7. Print out the accuracy of the model built

Further reading

To learn more about botnets and how to detect them with machine learning, I highly recommend you check out these useful external links:

- **How botnets expand and how to protect against them:** `https://bitninja.io/blog/2016/01/11/how-botnets-expand-and-how-protect-against-them`

- **Botnet basics – don't become a zombie!:** `https://blog.trendmicro.com/botnet-basics/`

- **Deep neural networks for bot detection:** `https://arxiv.org/abs/1802.04289`

- **Network-based Detection of IoT Botnet Attacks (N-BaIoT) using deep autoencoders:** `https://arxiv.org/abs/1805.03409`

- **A Hybrid Spectral Clustering and Deep Neural Network Ensemble Algorithm for Intrusion Detection in Sensor Networks** (`http://www.covert.io/research-papers/deep-learning-security/A%20Hybrid%20Spectral%20Clustering%20and%20Deep%20Neural%20Network%20Ensemble%20Algorithm%20for%20Intrusion%20Detection%20in%20Sensor%20Networks.pdf`)

- **An Analysis of Recurrent Neural Networks for Botnet Detection Behavior** (`http://www.covert.io/research-papers/deep-learning-security/An%20Analysis%20of%20Recurrent%20Neural%20Networks%20for%20Botnet%20Detection%20Behavior.pdf`)

Machine Learning in Anomaly Detection Systems

6

Unauthorized activity on a network can be a nightmare for any business. Protecting customers' data is the ultimate concern, and is the responsibility of every business owner. Deploying intrusion detection systems is a wise decision modern organizations can make to defend against malicious intrusions. Unfortunately, attackers and black hat hackers are always inventing new techniques to bypass protection, in order to gain unauthorized access to networks. That is why machine learning techniques are a good solution to protect networks from even sophisticated and attacks.

This chapter will be a one-stop guide for discovering network anomalies and learning how to build intrusion detection systems from scratch, using publicly available datasets and cutting-edge, open source Python data science libraries.

 In this chapter, we will cover the following:

- An overview of anomaly detection techniques
- Network attacks
- Detecting network anomalies
- **Host-based intrusion detection systems (HIDS)**
- **Network-based intrusion detection systems (NIDS)**

Technical requirements

These are the requirements needed in this chapter:

- A working knowledge of networking is required for this chapter.
- We are going to use the same Python libraries that we saw in earlier chapters, with the addition of a new library, called **Yellowbrick**. (You will find the installation instructions in this chapter.)
- You can find the code files used in this chapter in the GitHub repository at `https://github.com/PacktPublishing/Mastering-Machine-Learning-for-Penetration-Testing/tree/master/Chapter06`.

An overview of anomaly detection techniques

We will now discuss network anomalies (which are our prime concern) and their detection methods. By definition, an anomaly is something outside of the norm, an unexpected pattern in data. The term anomaly is used widely in data mining, and is sometimes called an outlier. Anomaly detection techniques are often used for fraud detection and to find malicious activities. In networking, anomalies can occur for many reasons, but what is important to us, in this case, is malicious activity detection. Generally, we see three types of anomalies:

- **Point anomalies**: Anomalous individual data instances, compared to the rest of the data.
- **Contextual anomalies**: Anomalous behaviors that occur only during specific contexts (periods of time, regions, and so on).
- **Collective anomalies**: A collection of anomalous activities, compared to the rest of the data.

These anomalies can be detected using many techniques, based on the data that is available.

Static rules technique

If we have training data, then we need to check that the data is balanced. If we don't have training data, the decision will be made based on the anomaly type; to detect point anomalies, it is recommended that you use percentiles and histograms. To detect collective anomalies, the decision will be based on the variance of the anomalies; to detect univariate anomalies, you can use Markov chains, or you can build a model and look at the residue. In a multivariate situation, we can use clustering and Markov models (if the anomalies are ordered) or k-Nearest-Neighbors (if the anomalies are unordered).

The different techniques are represented in the following diagram:

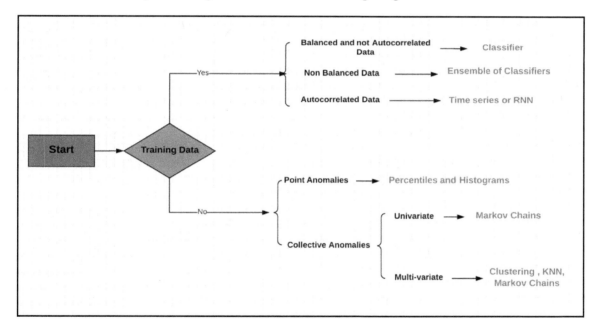

Network attacks taxonomy

When it comes to network anomalies, our job is protecting the organization's network from intruders. A network intrusion is a malicious activity that threatens the security of the network. Information security professionals have suggested many categorizations to classify network attacks for better study. For example, they have classified network attacks into the following:

- Infection (malware)
- Exploding (buffer overflow)
- Probing (sniffing)
- Cheating (spoofing)
- Traverse (brute-forcing)
- Concurrency (DDoS)

Attacks can also be categorized into passive and active attacks. An active attack is when the attacker has a direct effect on the network. The **Defense Advanced Research Projects Agency** (**DARPA**) has classified active attacks into four major categories, in its intrusion detection evaluation plan. The four categories are as follows:

- **Denial of Service (DoS)**: DoS attacks are attempts to interrupt an authorized user's access to the network. In other words, they block users from access to online services, like email.
- **User to Root (U2R) attacks**: U2R attacks are hard to detect; they attempt to gain high (superuser) privileges. This is achieved by accessing systems as normal users and trying to exploit the system's weaknesses later on, to escalate the privileges.
- **Remote to Local (R2L)**: An R2L attack is an attempt to interact with remote machines to gain access. One technique that is used is password guessing.
- **Probe**: A probe is an attempt to gain information about the hosts in the network, including valid IP addresses, running services, and open ports. It is usually done by scanning. As you know, the information gathered will later be used to identify vulnerabilities in order to exploit them.

The detection of network anomalies

Network **intrusion detection systems** (**IDSs**) are not a new idea. They have been proposed since the earliest network attacks. IDS can be categorized into two major categories, based on their deployment: HIDS and NIDS. The following diagram illustrates a high-level overview of an IDS architecture:

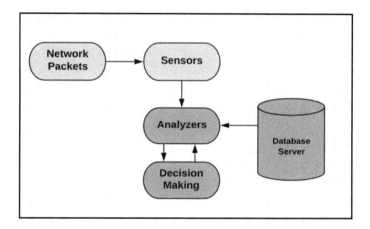

HIDS

HIDS are able to collect and monitor computer systems (especially their internals) in order to give security analysts a deep visibility into what's happening on critical systems, such as workstations, servers, and mobile devices. The main goal of an HIDS is to detect intrusions.

NIDS

NIDS are responsible for detecting intrusions in network data. Basically, the detection is made based on specific patterns in sequential data. In other words, NIDSs read all of the incoming packets and try to find anomalies in them.

Anomaly-based IDS

When it comes to IDS, we are generally talking about two categories: host-based and network-based. But a new class of IDS has also arisen. The new category is anomaly-based. These systems work by using machine learning techniques to identify intrusions and anomalies in data. In the previous chapters, especially in `Chapter 1`, *Introduction to Machine Learning in Pen Testing*, we looked at the different models of machine learning: supervised, unsupervised, semi-supervised, and reinforcement learning. Anomaly-based IDS are also categorized into supervised and unsupervised systems, depending on the machine learning model used to detect the network intrusion. The information security community, after many years of research, has succeeded in providing a classification of the different methods used in IDS. One of the proposals, called *Shallow and Deep Networks Intrusion Detection System: A Taxonomy and Survey*, delivered by Elike Hodo, Xavier J. A. Bellekens, Andrew Hamilton, Christos Tachtatzis, and Robert C. Atkinson, gives a detailed overview of many machine learning techniques for reliable intrusion detection. Some of the techniques are presented in the following diagram:

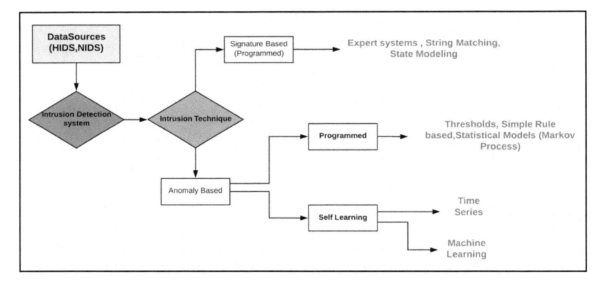

As you can see, we discussed many of the suggested techniques in previous chapters. Generally, in supervised anomaly detection, the input data and the anomaly classes are known. In other words, all of the data is labeled; even collecting labeled data is an exhausting and time-consuming task. The data that is captured will be processed before being sent to the detection engine. Unsupervised anomaly detection systems could be novel solutions while they are working even if the data is not labeled.

Clustering is one of the most common techniques used in unsupervised systems. The two different systems can be combined into one hybrid intrusion detection system. An overall hybrid anomaly intrusion detection system is shown here:

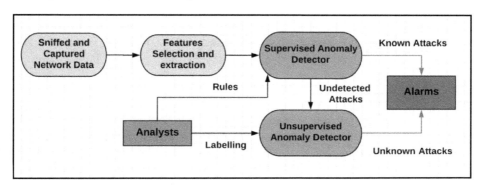

If you want to build a successful and reliable anomaly-based network intrusion detection system, you need to consider many important factors. One of these factors is proximity measure; by definition, proximity means a measurement of the similarity, or dissimilarity, of objects. Thus, as discussed previously, these systems are trying to classify or cluster data into groups and so respectively measuring the proximity of objects to one another. Similarity measures take values between 0 and 1, where 1 is the greatest similarity value. Euclidean distance and Manhattan distance are some common proximity measures. The selection of a suitable measure depends on the type of data (numeric or categorical). The anomalies are not detected arbitrarily, but are based on a scoring system. Sub-samples are marked by intrusion scores called **anomaly scores**. This scoring system is very beneficial to information security analysts; based on an ordered and ranked list of anomalies, they can select a threshold to work by, according to the severity. The following are some common anomaly scoring techniques used by anomaly network intrusion detection systems:

- **Distance-based anomaly score estimation**:
    - **Link-based outlier and anomaly detection in evolving datasets**: The dataset contains both continuous and categorical attributes. It uses a similarity metric to measure the link strength and the degree of association between two points.
    - **Reduced memory load**: This defines an anomaly as a data point that has subset attributes that take on unusual values.

- **Density-based anomaly score estimation**:
    - **Outlier detection for mixed attribute datasets**: This detects anomalies by computing the irregularity of values and the relationships between different types of attributes.

Building your own IDS

By now, you know the different network anomaly detection techniques. We are now going to build our own network IDS with Python, from scratch. The University of California hosted a competition called *The Third International Knowledge Discovery and Data Mining Tools Competition*, and they provided a dataset called **KDD Cup 1999 Data**, or **KDD 1990**. You can find it at http://kdd.ics.uci.edu/databases/kddcup99/kddcup99.html.

The main aim of the competition was building a system that was able to distinguish between bad (attack) and good (normal) connections. Many modern proposals and machine learning solutions were made using the dataset. But as you can see, the dataset is old; the models were not able to detect modern network attacks, in addition to other issues, like data redundancy. A great study called *A Detailed Analysis of the KDD CUP 99 Data Set*, done by Mahbod Tavallaee, Ebrahim Bagheri, Wei Lu, and Ali A. Ghorbani, highlighted many issues in the KDD99 dataset. A new dataset arose to solve the issues, named NSL-KDD (http://www.unb.ca/cic/datasets/nsl.html). Even that didn't solve all of the issues, but many improvements were made. The improvements reduced the data by about 75%.

These are some additional, publicly available datasets that can help you to build your own intrusion detection systems:

- **Coburg Intrusion Detection Data Sets (CIDDS)**: https://www.hs-coburg.de/index.php?id=927
- **UGR'16, A New Dataset for the Evaluation of Cyclostationarity-Based Network IDSs**: https://nesg.ugr.es/nesg-ugr16/index.php#CAL
- **Intrusion Detection Evaluation Dataset (CICIDS2017)**: http://www.unb.ca/cic/datasets/ids-2017.html

For our model, we are going to use the **NSL_KDD** as a dataset for training and testing. To get it, just clone it from GitHub, or simply use it directly, since we are providing all of the datasets discussed in this book in the book's GitHub repository. You can find it in the Chapter 06 folder:

```
# git clone https://github.com/defcom17/NSL_KDD
```

```
                          ghost@kali: ~/Desktop/Chapter6            ●  ▣  ✖
 File  Edit  View  Search  Terminal  Help
 ghost@kali:~/Desktop/Chapter6$ git clone https://github.com/defcom17/NSL_KDD
 Cloning into 'NSL_KDD'...
 remote: Counting objects: 15, done.
 remote: Total 15 (delta 0), reused 0 (delta 0), pack-reused 15
 Unpacking objects: 100% (15/15), done.
 Checking connectivity... done.
 ghost@kali:~/Desktop/Chapter6$ ls
 NSL_KDD
 ghost@kali:~/Desktop/Chapter6$ ls NSL_KDD
 20 Percent Training Set.csv  KDDTest+.csv         Original NSL KDD Zip.zip
 Attack Types.csv             KDDTest+.txt         ReadMe.txt
 Field Names.csv              KDDTrain+_20Percent.txt  Small Training Set.csv
 Field Names.docx             KDDTrain+.csv
 KDDTest-21.txt               KDDTrain+.txt
 ghost@kali:~/Desktop/Chapter6$ █
```

The dataset contains different files:

- `KDDTrain+.arff`: The full NSL-KDD training set, with binary labels in ARFF format.
- `KDDTrain+.txt`: The full NSL-KDD training set, including attack-type labels and difficulty levels in CSV format.
- `KDDTrain+_20Percent.ARFF`: A 20% subset of the `KDDTrain+.arff` file.
- `KDDTrain+_20Percent.TXT`: A 20% subset of the `KDDTrain+.txt` file.
- `KDDTest+.ARFF`: The full NSL-KDD test set, with binary labels in ARFF format.
- `KDDTest+.TXT`: The full NSL-KDD test set, including attack-type labels and difficulty levels in CSV format.
- `KDDTest-21.ARFF`: A subset of the `KDDTest+.arff` file, which does not include records, with difficulty levels of 21 out of 21.
- `KDDTest-21.TXT`: A subset of the `KDDTest+.txt` file, which does not include records, with difficulty levels of 21 out of 21.

If you open `Field Names.csv`, you will see all of the 40 fields:

duration	continuous
protocol_type	symbolic
service	symbolic
flag	symbolic
src_bytes	continuous
dst_bytes	continuous
land	continuous
wrong_fragment	continuous
urgent	continuous
hot	continuous
num_failed_logins	continuous
logged_in	continuous
num_compromised	continuous
root_shell	continuous
su_attempted	continuous
num_root	continuous
num_file_creations	continuous
rerror_rate	continuous
srv_rerror_rate	continuous
same_srv_rate	continuous
diff_srv_rate	continuous
srv_diff_host_rate	continuous
dst_host_count	continuous
dst_host_srv_count	continuous
dst_host_same_srv_rate	continuous
dst_host_diff_srv_rate	continuous
dst_host_same_src_port_rate	continuous
dst_host_srv_diff_host_rate	continuous
dst_host_serror_rate	continuous
dst_host_srv_serror_rate	continuous
dst_host_rerror_rate	continuous
dst_host_srv_rerror_rate	continuous

To import this dataset, we will use `pandas`:

```
>>> import pandas as pd
>>> Data = pd.read_csv("KDDTrain+.csv", header=None)
```

If we check the columns with `Data.columns`, we will see that the columns, or fields, are represented as numbers:

```
                        ghost@kali: ~/Desktop/Chapter6/NSL_KDD
 File  Edit  View  Search  Terminal  Help
>>> import pandas as pd
>>> Data = pd.read_csv("KDDTrain+.csv", header=None)
>>> Data.columns
Int64Index([ 0,  1,  2,  3,  4,  5,  6,  7,  8,  9, 10, 11, 12, 13, 14, 15, 16,
            17, 18, 19, 20, 21, 22, 23, 24, 25, 26, 27, 28, 29, 30, 31, 32, 33,
            34, 35, 36, 37, 38, 39, 40, 41, 42],
           dtype='int64')
>>>
```

To make our feature analysis easier, let's assign a field name to a number for better feature representation. To do that, we will create an array called `Columns`, filled with field names, and load the dataset with it:

```
Columns = ["duration","protocol_type","service","flag","src_bytes",
"dst_bytes","land","wrong_fragment","urgent","hot","num_failed_logins",
    "logged_in","num_compromised","root_shell","su_attempted","num_root",
"num_file_creations","num_shells","num_access_files","num_outbound_cmds",
    "is_host_login","is_guest_login","count","srv_count","serror_rate",
    "srv_serror_rate","rerror_rate","srv_rerror_rate","same_srv_rate",
"diff_srv_rate","srv_diff_host_rate","dst_host_count","dst_host_srv_count",
"dst_host_same_srv_rate","dst_host_diff_srv_rate","dst_host_same_src_port_r
ate",
"dst_host_srv_diff_host_rate","dst_host_serror_rate","dst_host_srv_serror_r
ate",
"dst_host_rerror_rate","dst_host_srv_rerror_rate","label","difficulty"]
```

Load the data:

```
Data = pd.read_csv("KDDTrain+.csv", header=None, names = Columns)
Data.columns
```

These are the feature names:

```
ghost@kali: ~/Desktop/Chapter6/NSL_KDD
File  Edit  View  Search  Terminal  Help
>>> Data.columns
Index([u'duration', u'protocol_type', u'service', u'flag', u'src_bytes',
       u'dst_bytes', u'land', u'wrong_fragment', u'urgent', u'hot',
       u'num_failed_logins', u'logged_in', u'num_compromised', u'root_shell',
       u'su_attempted', u'num_root', u'num_file_creations', u'num_shells',
       u'num_access_files', u'num_outbound_cmds', u'is_host_login',
       u'is_guest_login', u'count', u'srv_count', u'serror_rate',
       u'srv_serror_rate', u'rerror_rate', u'srv_rerror_rate',
       u'same_srv_rate', u'diff_srv_rate', u'srv_diff_host_rate',
       u'dst_host_count', u'dst_host_srv_count', u'dst_host_same_srv_rate',
       u'dst_host_diff_srv_rate', u'dst_host_same_src_port_rate',
       u'dst_host_srv_diff_host_rate', u'dst_host_serror_rate',
       u'dst_host_srv_serror_rate', u'dst_host_rerror_rate',
       u'dst_host_srv_rerror_rate', u'label', u'difficulty'],
      dtype='object')
>>>
```

To better understand the dataset, we can use `pandas.DataFrame.describe`:

```
Data.describe()
```

```
ghost@kali: ~/Desktop/Chapter6/NSL_KDD
File  Edit  View  Search  Terminal  Help
>>> Data.describe()
            duration       src_bytes       dst_bytes            land  \
count  125973.00000    1.259730e+05    1.259730e+05   125973.000000
mean      287.14465    4.556674e+04    1.977911e+04        0.000198
std      2604.51531    5.870331e+06    4.021269e+06        0.014086
min         0.00000    0.000000e+00    0.000000e+00        0.000000
25%         0.00000    0.000000e+00    0.000000e+00        0.000000
50%         0.00000    4.400000e+01    0.000000e+00        0.000000
75%         0.00000    2.760000e+02    5.160000e+02        0.000000
max     42908.00000    1.379964e+09    1.309937e+09        1.000000

       wrong_fragment          urgent             hot  num_failed_logins  \
count    125973.000000   125973.000000   125973.000000      125973.000000
mean          0.022687        0.000111        0.204409           0.001222
std           0.253530        0.014366        2.149968           0.045239
min           0.000000        0.000000        0.000000           0.000000
25%           0.000000        0.000000        0.000000           0.000000
50%           0.000000        0.000000        0.000000           0.000000
```

Before training the model, some additional processing is needed.
`sklearn.preprocessing.LabelEncoder` encodes labels with values between 0 and
`n_classes-1` and `fit_transform(y)`. Fit the label encoder and return encoded labels. In
our case, we are transforming non-numerical labels into numerical labels. Also, we need to
pre-process four labels: `protocol_type`, `service`, `flag`, and `label`.

To do that, we use `fit.transform()`, which calibrates our measurements:

```
from sklearn import preprocessing

Data.protocol_type =
preprocessing.LabelEncoder().fit_transform(Data["protocol_type"])
  Data.service = preprocessing.LabelEncoder().fit_transform(Data["service"])
  Data.flag = preprocessing.LabelEncoder().fit_transform(Data["flag"])
  Data.label = preprocessing.LabelEncoder().fit_transform(Data["label"])
```

```
                    ghost@kali: ~/Desktop/Chapter6/NSL_KDD                    ● ● ⊗
File  Edit  View  Search  Terminal  Help
>>> Data.protocol_type = preprocessing.LabelEncoder().fit_transform(Data["protocol_type"])
>>> Data.service = preprocessing.LabelEncoder().fit_transform(Data["service"])
>>> Data.flag = preprocessing.LabelEncoder().fit_transform(Data["flag"])
>>> Data.label = preprocessing.LabelEncoder().fit_transform(Data["label"])
>>> Data.protocol_type
0      1
1      2
2      1
3      1
4      1
5      1
6      1
7      1
8      1
9      1
10     1
11     1
12     1
```

 In scikit-learn, there are two different methods: `fit` and `fit_transform`. The difference between the two methods is that `fit` calculates the parameters (μ and σ, where μ is the mean of the population and σ is the standard deviation of the population) and saves them internally, while `fit_transform` does the same task but also applies a transformation to a particular set of samples.

Let's identify our data. In the following lines, we have used an additional NumPy method, `as_matrix()`, to convert the frame to its NumPy-array representation. In a NumPy-array, the return is not a NumPy matrix, but a NumPy array, according to the official documentation:

```
X = Data[Columns].as_matrix()
y = Data.label.as_matrix()
```

Usually, after this step, we would perform the model training; but this time, we are going to take more time to analyze and visualize our data and features. One of the tasks of data science is obtaining insights and knowledge, and visualization is essential to data science and machine learning. My recommendation is to play with data as much as you can, and poke around with different techniques. As you will have noticed, a machine learning system generally respects the same techniques, and your job, as a data scientist or machine learning expert, is to select the right features from the data. Machine learning algorithms are based on mathematics, and usually, you are not going to change the algorithm itself; instead, you'll want to perform some good feature engineering to build a reliable and good model with high accuracy that meets your goals.

Yellowbrick is a great visualization library and suite of visual diagnostic tools (visualizers). This library depends on scikit-learn and Matplotlib. You can install it by using `pip`:

```
pip install yellowbrick
```

This library is very rich, letting you visualize features, classification, regression, clustering, and even text (for example, visualizing the frequency distribution of terms in a corpus):

```
visualizer = Rank1D(features=Columns, algorithm='shapiro')
visualizer.fit(X, y)
visualizer.transform(X)
visualizer.poof()
```

```
ghost@kali: ~/Desktop/Chapter6/NSL_KDD

File  Edit  View  Search  Terminal  Help

>>> from yellowbrick.features.rankd import Rank1D, Rank2D
>>> X = Data[Columns].as_matrix()
>>> y = Data.label.as_matrix()
>>> visualizer = Rank1D(features=Columns, algorithm='shapiro')
>>> visualizer.fit(X, y)
Rank1D(algorithm=None,
    ax=<matplotlib.axes._subplots.AxesSubplot object at 0x7f557b881f10>,
    features=None, orient=None, show_feature_names=None)
>>> visualizer.transform(X)
/usr/local/lib/python2.7/dist-packages/scipy/stats/morestats.py:1326: UserWarning: p-value may not be accur
ate for N > 5000.
  warnings.warn("p-value may not be accurate for N > 5000.")
/usr/local/lib/python2.7/dist-packages/scipy/stats/morestats.py:1323: UserWarning: Input data for shapiro h
as range zero. The results may not be accurate.
  warnings.warn("Input data for shapiro has range zero. The results "
array([[ 0.,  1., 20., ...,  0., 11., 20.],
       [ 0.,  2., 44., ...,  0., 11., 15.],
       [ 0.,  1., 49., ...,  0.,  9., 19.],
       ...,
       [ 0.,  1., 54., ...,  0., 11., 18.],
       [ 0.,  1., 30., ...,  0.,  9., 20.],
       [ 0.,  1., 20., ...,  0., 11., 21.]])
>>> visualizer.poof()
```

`visualizer.poof()` will display the plot as follows:

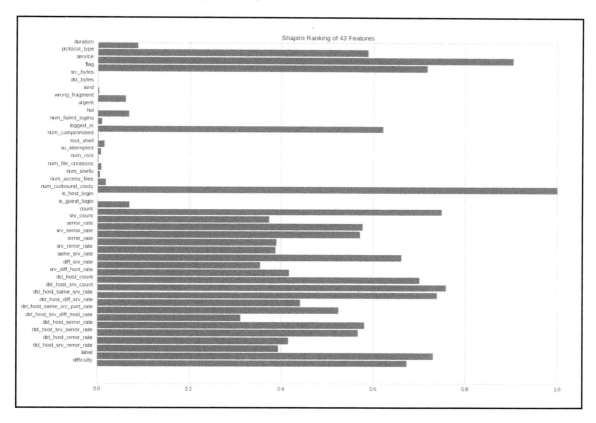

To save the plot, you can add `outpath`, like in the following:

```
visualizer.poof(outpath="Figure1.png")
```

You can even export it as a PDF file. You may have noticed that in the line `visualizer = Rank1D(features=Columns, algorithm='shapiro')`, we used a method called `Rank1D` and an algorithm called `shapiro`, to rank features and detect the relationships between them. `Rank1D` and `Rank2D` evaluate single features or pairs of features. In our case, we used a one-dimensional ranking of features.

`Rank2D` is a two-dimensional ranking of features. The following shows how to implement it:

```
visualizer = Rank2D(features=Columns, algorithm='covariance')
```

You can select from `pearson` or `covariance`:

```
visualizer.fit(X, y)
visualizer.transform(X)
visualizer.poof()
```

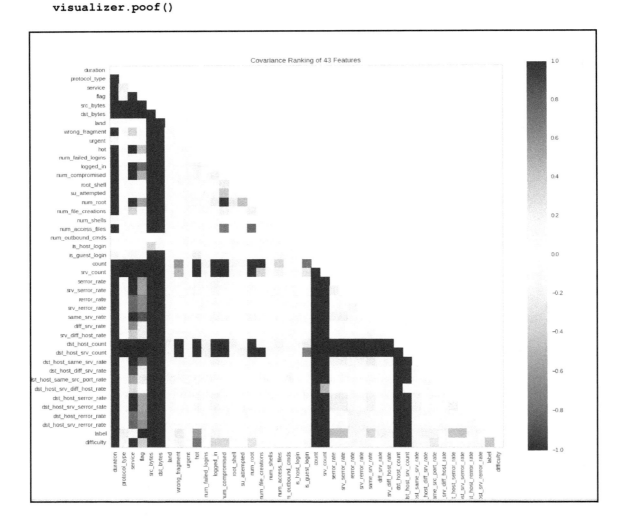

Let's go back to the ranking algorithms we used. The `shapiro` parameter refers to the Shapiro-Wilk ranking algorithm. You can select your ranking algorithm:

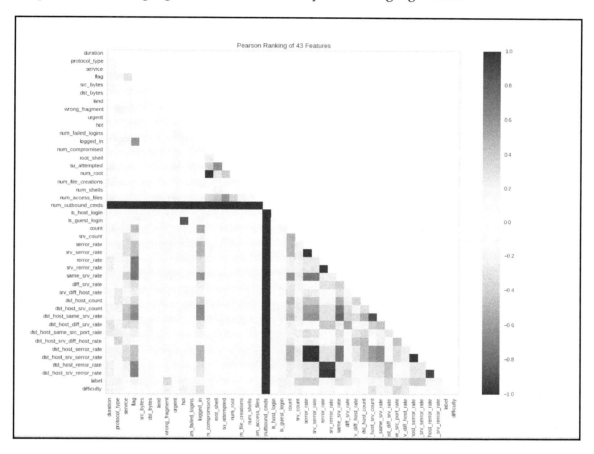

We previously discovered **Principal Component Analysis (PCA)**. Yellowbrick gives you the ability to decompose high-dimensional data into two or three dimensions, and plot them:

```
visualizer = PCADecomposition(scale=True, center=False, col=y)
visualizer.fit_transform(X,y)
visualizer.poof()
```

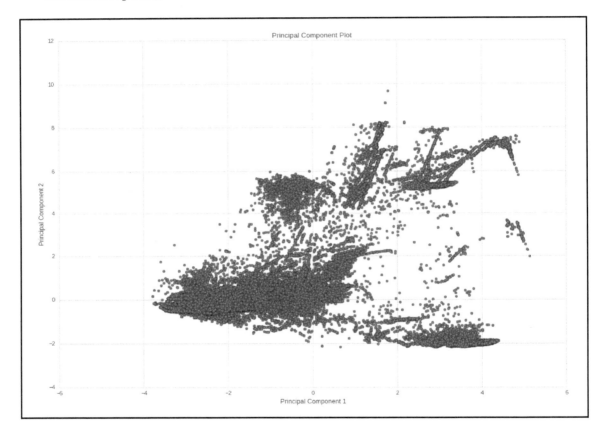

Also, the plot can be in 3D:

```
visualizer = PCADecomposition(scale=True, center=False, color=y,
proj_dim=3)
 visualizer.fit_transform(X,y)
 visualizer.poof()
```

The preceding code is presented in this graph:

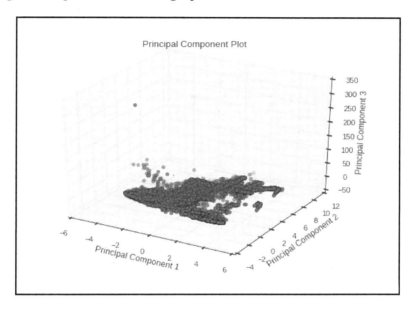

Now it is time to train our intrusion detection machine learning model. As usual, we split the data, select the classifier used, fit the model, and get the scoring results:

```
clf = RandomForestClassifier(max_depth=2, random_state=0)
clf.fit(X, y)
Score = clf.score(X_test,y_test)
print(Score*100)
```

```
ghost@kali: ~/Desktop/Chapter6/NSL_KDD
File  Edit  View  Search  Terminal  Help
>>> X_train, X_test, y_train, y_test = train_test_split(X, y, test_size=0.2)
>>> clf.fit(X, y)
RandomForestClassifier(bootstrap=True, class_weight=None, criterion='gini',
            max_depth=2, max_features='auto', max_leaf_nodes=None,
            min_impurity_decrease=0.0, min_impurity_split=None,
            min_samples_leaf=1, min_samples_split=2,
            min_weight_fraction_leaf=0.0, n_estimators=10, n_jobs=1,
            oob_score=False, random_state=0, verbose=0, warm_start=False)
>>> Score = clf.score(X_test,y_test)
>>> print (Score*100)
85.75511014090097
>>>
```

The score of our intrusion detection system is 85.7%. For more details, you can output the evaluation metrics (TF, FP, TN, FN, and Recall), as done in the previous models.

The Kale stack

Monitoring is a difficult mission, especially when it comes to a team of hundreds of engineers, where metrics overload can occur. To solve this problem, in addition to a time series-based anomaly detection ability, there are many projects that we can use. One of them is the Kale stack. It consists of two parts: Skyline and Oculus. The role of Skyline is to detect anomalous metrics (an anomaly detection system), while Oculus is the anomaly correlation component. To download the two components, you can check the following repositories:

- Skyline: `http://github.com/etsy/skyline`
- Oculus: `http://github.com/etsy/oculus`

You will need the following:

- At least 8 GB RAM
- Quad Core Xeon 5620 CPU, or comparable
- 1 GB disk space

Summary

In this chapter, we explored the fundamentals of network anomaly detection techniques, and the theories behind them. You learned how to build a machine learning based network anomaly detector with Python. There are many other techniques that you can use to build a machine learning IDS. The next chapter will enhance your skills by guiding you through deploying a fully-working threat hunting platform, using an amazing stack for open source projects called the ELK stack.

Questions

1. What is an anomaly?
2. What is a Markov chain?
3. What are hidden Markov models?
4. How can we detect anomalies with hidden Markov models?
5. What's the difference between time series anomaly detection and the other types of anomaly detection?
6. What's the difference between time series anomaly detection and other types of anomaly detection?
7. What's the difference between supervised and unsupervised machine learning anomaly detection?

Further reading

- **Blog posts:**
  - **Anomaly detection articles:** https://www.kdnuggets.com/tag/anomaly-detection
  - **A practical guide to anomaly detection for DevOps:** https://www.bigpanda.io/blog/a-practical-guide-to-anomaly-detection/
- **Papers:**
  - **Root-Cause Analysis for Time-Series Anomalies via Spatiotemporal Graphical Modeling in Distributed Complex Systems:** https://arxiv.org/abs/1805.12296
  - **A Generalized Active Learning Approach for Unsupervised Anomaly Detection:** https://arxiv.org/abs/1805.09411
  - **Towards Explaining Anomalies: A Deep Taylor Decomposition of One-Class Models:** https://arxiv.org/abs/1805.06230
  - **Towards an Efficient Anomaly-Based Intrusion Detection for Software-Defined Networks:** https://arxiv.org/abs/1803.06762

7
Detecting Advanced Persistent Threats

Modern organizations face cyber threats on a daily basis. Black hat hackers do not show any indication that they are going to stop. New hacking techniques appear regularly. Detecting **advanced persistent threats** (**APTs**) is a hard mission, since the goals of these attacks are to stay undetected for a long period of time, and to steal data, rather than cause damage to systems.

According to multiple information security reports, the number of APT attacks is increasing in a notable way, targeting national defenses, manufacturing, and the financial industry. Thus, classic protection techniques are, in many cases, useless. Deploying suitable platforms and solutions can help organizations and companies defend against cyber attacks, especially APTs.

This chapter will give you step-by-step guidance to teach you how to build a threat-hunting platform, using a stack of well known open-source projects to protect your clients' data. You will learn how to create a machine learning module to enhance your platform and automate anomaly detection, so that you can focus on other concerns within your team.

In this chapter, we will cover:

- The advanced threat landscape
- Threat-hunting methodologies
- The hunting maturity model
- The cyber kill chain
- The diamond model of intrusion detection
- Threat hunting using machine learning, with the **Elasticsearch**, **Logstash**, and **Kibana** (**ELK**) stack

Technical requirements

In this chapter, we will use the same Python libraries that we used in the previous chapters. It is recommended that you have the following:

- 4 GB RAM
- 2 GB CPU

Threats and risk analysis

Threats are potential dangers to the assets of your organization. According to the **European Union Agency for Network and Information Security (ENISA)** Threat Landscape Report, 2017, modern organizations face millions of cyber threats, including: malware, web-based attacks, phishing, ransomware, botnets, and so on. For security professionals, and especially for risk managers, threats play a huge role in analyzing risks. Risks are a combination of threats and vulnerabilities, and they can be mathematically represented as *Risk = Threats x Vulnerability*.

Threat-hunting methodology

Threat hunting is an approach for search out, identifying, and understanding APTs. Threat hunting, like any methodological information security mission, is not about tools and utilities. It is a combination of processes, people, and technology.

Threat hunting involves the following steps:

- Creating hypotheses
- Investigating by using tools and techniques
- Uncovering new patterns
- Informing and enriching analytics

The following steps form the **threat-hunting loop**:

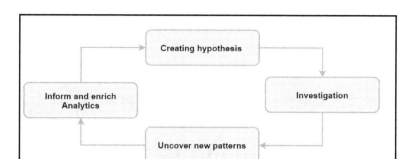

You can evaluate the maturity of your threat-hunting program by selecting a level from the following:

- **Level 1**: Initial (little or no data collection, relying on automated alerts)
- **Level 2**: Minimal (high level of data collection)
- **Level 3**: Procedural (high level of data collection, following data analysis procedures)
- **Level 4**: Innovative (high level of data collection, following new data analysis procedures)
- **Level 5**: Leading (high level of data collection, automating the successful data analysis procedures)

The following two sections include the most important terminologies in threat hunting.

The cyber kill chain

Like many aspects of information security, the cyber kill chain is a military-inspired model to describe the steps used in a cyber attack.

The seven steps of the cyber kill chain are as follows:

- **Reconnaissance**: Harvesting information, such as email addresses
- **Weaponization**: Coupling exploits with backdoors into a deliverable payload—in other words, building a deliverable payload using an exploit and a backdoor

- **Delivery**: Delivering a weaponized bundle to the victim via different means, such as an email or USB
- **Exploitation**: Exploiting a vulnerability to execute code on the targeted machine
- **Installation**: Installing a malware
- **Command and control (C2)**: Command channel for remote manipulation of the victim
- **Actions and objectives**: Accomplishing the original goal

The diamond model of intrusion analysis

The diamond model of intrusion analysis is a methodology that was developed to verify cyber threats. Every incident can be represented as a diamond. This cognitive model is used by many information security analysts to characterize organized threats consistently and track them as they evolve.

The four nodes of the diamond are as follows:

- Adversary (bad guy persona)
- Infrastructure (such as IP addresses, domain names, and email addresses)
- Capabilities (such as malware, exploits, and stolen certs)
- Victims (such as people and network assets)

Threat hunting with the ELK Stack

You have now seen a clear overview of the most important terminologies in threat hunting. So, let's build our threat-hunting platform. In the following sections, we will learn how to build a threat-hunting system by using open-source projects. In our hands-on guide, we will use one of the most promising solutions available—the ELK Stack. It includes three open-source projects, and is one of the most downloaded log management platforms nowadays.

The ELK Stack is widely used in many fields, including:

- Business intelligence
- Web analytics
- Information security
- Compliance

The ELK Stack is composed of the following components:

- **Elasticsearch**: To search and analyze data
- **Logstash**: To collect and transform data
- **Kibana**: To visualize data

The following diagram illustrates the major components in the ELK Stack:

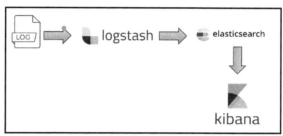

So, according to the main architecture, in order to build a threat-hunting platform, we need to: collect logs, analyze and search for suitable data, and manage a visualization of our findings. Let's look at how we can prepare the ELK Stack environment.

Elasticsearch

Elasticsearch is an amazing open-source project. It is a RESTful, distributed, and JSON-based search engine. In other words, you can look at it as a NoSQL search server. You can see its official website at `https://www.elastic.co/`:

To download it, go to `https://www.elastic.co/downloads/elasticsearch`:

Select a suitable package. In my case, I am going to install it on an Ubuntu 14.04 machine. Thus, I am going to select the `.deb` version. It is recommended that you have the following:

- 4GB RAM
- 2GB CPU

Elasticsearch is written in Java. So, we need to make sure that it is installed in our environment (we should download it if it is not). Add Java to the `apt` as follows:

```
sudo add-apt-repository -y ppa:webupd8team/java
```

Now Java source is added into the `list.sources` file:

Update the `list.sources` file:

```
                              azureuser@ELKStack: ~
 File  Edit  View  Search  Terminal  Help
azureuser@ELKStack:~$ sudo apt-get update
Ign http://azure.archive.ubuntu.com trusty InRelease
Get:1 http://azure.archive.ubuntu.com trusty-updates InRelease [65.9 kB]
Hit http://azure.archive.ubuntu.com trusty-backports InRelease
Hit http://azure.archive.ubuntu.com trusty Release.gpg
Hit http://azure.archive.ubuntu.com trusty Release
Get:2 http://azure.archive.ubuntu.com trusty-updates/main Sources [415 kB]
Get:3 http://azure.archive.ubuntu.com trusty-updates/restricted Sources [6,322 B]
Get:4 http://azure.archive.ubuntu.com trusty-updates/universe Sources [199 kB]
Get:5 http://azure.archive.ubuntu.com trusty-updates/multiverse Sources [7,368 B]
Get:6 http://azure.archive.ubuntu.com trusty-updates/main amd64 Packages [1,065 kB]
Get:7 http://azure.archive.ubuntu.com trusty-updates/restricted amd64 Packages [17.2 kB]
Get:8 http://azure.archive.ubuntu.com trusty-updates/universe amd64 Packages [449 kB]
Get:9 http://azure.archive.ubuntu.com trusty-updates/multiverse amd64 Packages [14.6 kB]
Get:10 http://azure.archive.ubuntu.com trusty-updates/main Translation-en [525 kB]
Get:11 http://azure.archive.ubuntu.com trusty-updates/multiverse Translation-en [7,616 B]
```

Now, install the Java `installer`:

```
sudo apt-get -y install oracle-java8-installer
```

```
                              azureuser@ELKStack: ~
 File  Edit  View  Search  Terminal  Help
azureuser@ELKStack:~$ sudo apt-get -y install oracle-java8-installer
Reading package lists... Done
Building dependency tree
Reading state information... Done
The following extra packages will be installed:
  binutils gsfonts gsfonts-x11 java-common libfontenc1 libxfont1
  oracle-java8-set-default x11-common xfonts-encodings xfonts-utils
Suggested packages:
  binutils-doc default-jre equivs binfmt-support visualvm ttf-baekmuk
  ttf-unfonts ttf-unfonts-core ttf-kochi-gothic ttf-sazanami-gothic
  ttf-kochi-mincho ttf-sazanami-mincho ttf-arphic-uming firefox firefox-2
  iceweasel mozilla-firefox iceape-browser mozilla-browser epiphany-gecko
  epiphany-webkit epiphany-browser galeon midbrowser moblin-web-browser
  xulrunner xulrunner-1.9 konqueror chromium-browser midori google-chrome
The following NEW packages will be installed:
  binutils gsfonts gsfonts-x11 java-common libfontenc1 libxfont1
  oracle-java8-installer oracle-java8-set-default x11-common xfonts-encodings
```

Then, configure it:

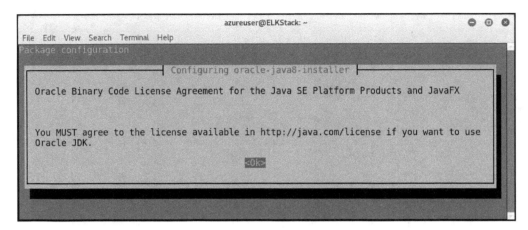

Voilà! We have installed it successfully. Check it by typing the `java -version` command:

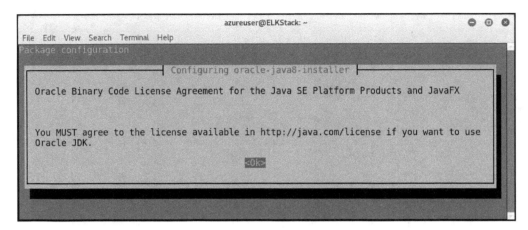

Let's install Elasticsearch. Import the `elasticsearch` public key as follows:

```
wget -qO - https://packages.elastic.co/GPG-KEY-elasticsearch | sudo
apt-key add -
```

Add Elasticsearch to the source list:

```
echo "deb https://artifacts.elastic.co/packages/6.x/apt stable main" |
sudo tee -a /etc/apt/sources.list.d/elastic-6.x.list
```

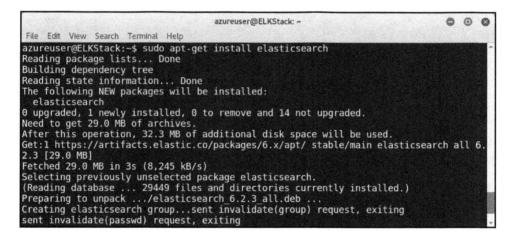

Update the source list by using `apt-get update` and `install elasticsearch`:

```
apt-get install elasticsearch
```

To configure Elasticsearch, edit `/etc/elasticsearch/elasticsearch.yml` by using a text editor:

```
vi /etc/elasticsearch/elasticsearch.yml
```

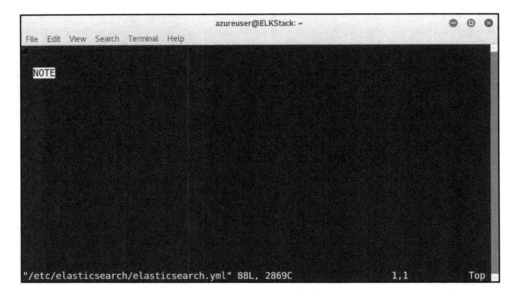

After configuring the file, restart the Elasticsearch service:

```
sudo service elasticsearch restart
```

Kibana

After installing and configuring Elasticsearch, it is time to install Kibana, to visualize data in a well-designed dashboard. Kibana is a web interface with different types of charts. You can see it as the visualization layer of our stack.

Install Kibana by using the `apt-get install` command, as usual:

```
apt-get install kibana
```

It won't take so long to install it:

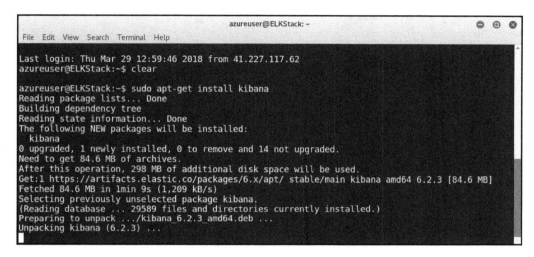

After installing it, we can configure it by using a text editor to modify the
/opt/kibana/config/kibana.yml configuration file:

```
sudo vi /opt/kibana/config/kibana.yml
```

Enable the Kibana service by using the following command:

```
sudo update-rc.d kibana defaults 96 9
```

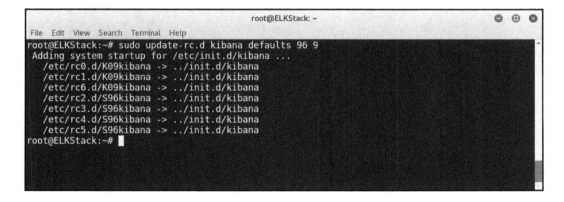

Start the service by using the following command:

```
sudo service kibana start
```

If you want to access the dashboard from outside using a public IP address, you can use a reverse proxy. For example, **Nginx** would be great in this case.

You can find the Kibana folders at /usr/share/kibana:

```
root@ELKStack:~# cd /usr/share/kibana
root@ELKStack:/usr/share/kibana# ls
bin            node modules  package.json  src
LICENSE.txt   NOTICE.txt     plugins       ui framework
node          optimize       README.txt    webpackShims
root@ELKStack:/usr/share/kibana#
```

To check the dashboard, type `<Address>: 5601` and enter your credentials:

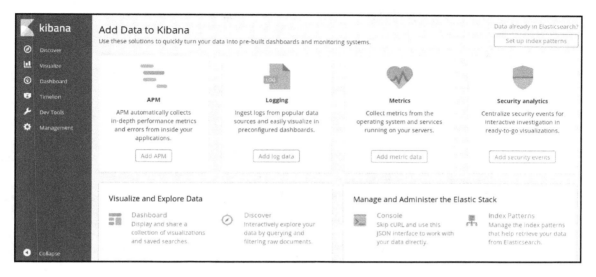

Logstash

At this point, we have installed Elasticsearch and Kibana; now we need to install Logstash to collect and transform data. The Logstash pipeline contains three components:

- Input
- Filters
- Output

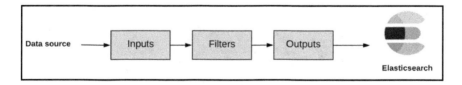

Let's add Logstash to the sources list, and then update it:

```
echo 'deb http://packages.elastic.co/logstash/2.2/debian stable main' |
sudo tee /etc/apt/sources.list.d/logstash-2.2.x.list
```

Install Logstash as follows:

```
apt-get install logstash
```

Once you have installed Logstash, you can edit its configuration
file, `<Parent_Directory>/logstash/conf/logstash.conf`. As you will notice, the
configuration file contains two sections - `input` and `output`:

```
                        bitnami@ELK1: ~/stack/logstash/conf              ⊖  ⊚  ⊗

 File  Edit  View  Search  Terminal  Help

input
{
    beats
    {
        ssl => false
        host => "0.0.0.0"
        port => 5044
    }
    gelf
    {
        host => "0.0.0.0"
        port => 12201
    }
    http
    {
        ssl => false
                                                      1,0-1           Top
```

Wait! I bet you are wondering why we only have two sections, even though Logstash
contains three sections, as we discussed before. You are totally right. We need to add a
customized section, called `filters`. Logstash provides good capabilities, including the
ability to create personalized filters. For example, to create a filter, you can use the
following format (we will use it later, in our guide):

```
filter {
    grok {
        match => { "message" => "COMBINEDAPACHELOG %{COMMONAPACHELOG}
%{QS:referrer} %{QS:agent}" }
    }
    date {
        match => [ "timestamp" , "dd/MMM/yyyy:HH:mm:ss Z" ]
    }
}
```

The `gork` filter is used to parse unstructured log data into something structured and
queryable. According to the official section on filter plugins (https://www.elastic.co/
guide/en/logstash/current/plugins-filters-grok.html), Logstash delivers more than
120 patterns, by default.

Machine learning with the ELK Stack using the X-Pack plugin

We have now installed the three main components of an ELK Stack. If you want an efficient way to deploy an ELK Stack, especially for testing purposes, I recommend that you use a cloud-based stack. For example, in the following demonstrations, I am going to use a predefined cloud ELK Stack by Bitnami.

The Bitnami ELK Stack ships with the following software versions:

- Apache 2.4.29
- Elasticsearch 6.2.2
- Logstash 6.2.2
- Kibana 6.2.2

In a few moments, your stack will be ready to use. The following screenshot shows the ELK Stack files:

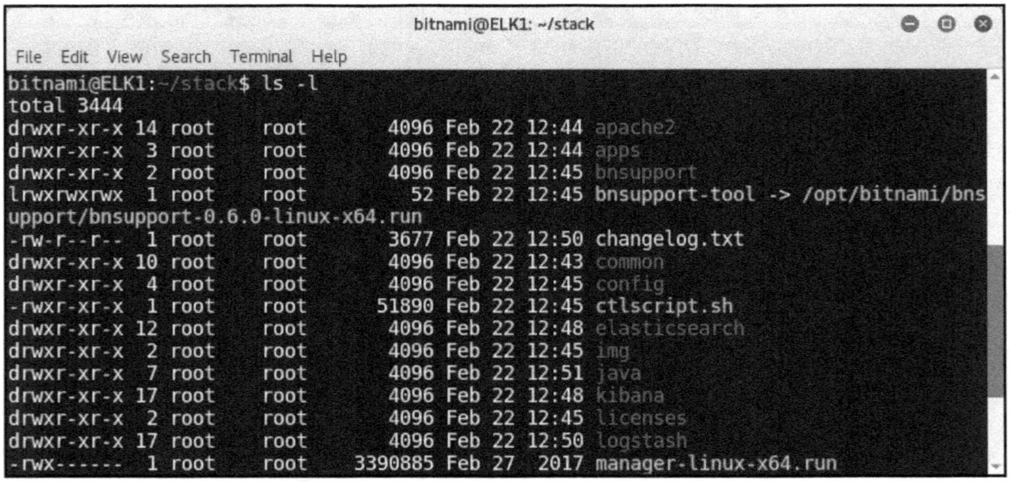

To get the password for your Bitnami environment, go to the **Boot diagnostics** section in your Azure portal, and check the log file; you will find the password at the bottom of the file:

```
[ ][0;32m OK  ][0m] Started Snappy daemon.
[   36.681718] bitnami1[1549]: ############################################################
[   36.695733] bitnami1[1549]: #                                                          #
[   36.722314] bitnami1[1549]: #       Setting Bitnami application password to 'E7DRnqi1OAJp'
[   36.747684] bitnami1[1549]: #       (the default application username is 'user')        #
[   36.783504] bitnami1[1549]: #                                                          #
[   36.817251] bitnami1[1549]: ############################################################
[   37.628951] bitnami1[1549]: [Tue Apr  3 12:47:20 UTC 2018] Regenerating keys for apache2
[   38.204812] cloud-init[1386]: Cloud-init v. 17.1 running 'modules:config' at Tue, 03 Apr 2018 12:47:13 +0000. Up 31.47 secon
```

Before adding the machine learning plugin, let's configure our ELK Stack. Load the ELK environment and log in to the ELK server using the following command:

```
sudo /opt/bitnami/use_elk
```

```
bitnami@ELK1: /opt/bitnami
File  Edit  View  Search  Terminal  Help
bitnami@ELK1:~$ cd  /opt/bitnami/
bitnami@ELK1:/opt/bitnami$ ls
apache2         changelog.txt   img        manager-linux-x64.run  use_elk
apps            common          java       properties.ini         var
bitnami         config          kibana     README.txt
bnsupport       ctlscript.sh    licenses   scripts
bnsupport-tool  elasticsearch   logstash   stats
bitnami@ELK1:/opt/bitnami$ ./use_elk
-bash: ./use_elk: Permission denied
bitnami@ELK1:/opt/bitnami$ sudo ./use_elk
bash-4.3#
```

Let's stop Logstash by typing `sudo /opt/bitnami/ctlscript.sh stop logstash`

```
bitnami@ELK1: /opt/bitnami
File  Edit  View  Search  Terminal  Help
bitnami@ELK1:~$ cd  /opt/bitnami/
bitnami@ELK1:/opt/bitnami$ ls
apache2         changelog.txt   img        manager-linux-x64.run  use_elk
apps            common          java       properties.ini         var
bitnami         config          kibana     README.txt
bnsupport       ctlscript.sh    licenses   scripts
bnsupport-tool  elasticsearch   logstash   stats
bitnami@ELK1:/opt/bitnami$ ./use_elk
-bash: ./use_elk: Permission denied
bitnami@ELK1:/opt/bitnami$ sudo ./use_elk
bash-4.3# sudo /opt/bitnami/ctlscript.sh stop logstash
Unmonitored logstash
/opt/bitnami/logstash/scripts/ctl.sh : logstash stopped
bash-4.3#
```

Create a configuration file, `/opt/bitnami/logstash/conf/access-log.conf`:

```
input {
    file {
        path => "/opt/bitnami/apache2/logs/access_log"
        start_position => beginning
    }
}
filter {
    grok {
        match => { "message" => "COMBINEDAPACHELOG %{COMMONAPACHELOG}
%{QS:referrer} %{QS:agent}" }
    }
    date {
        match => [ "timestamp" , "dd/MMM/yyyy:HH:mm:ss Z" ]
    }
}

output {
    elasticsearch {
        hosts => [ "127.0.0.1:9200" ]
    }
}
```

```
                          bitnami@ELK1: /opt/bitnami                        ─  □  ✖
File  Edit  View  Search  Terminal  Help
input {
    file {
        path => "/opt/bitnami/apache2/logs/access_log"
        start_position => beginning
    }
}

filter {
    grok {
        match => { "message" => "COMBINEDAPACHELOG %{COMMONAPACHELOG} %{QS:referrer} %{QS:agent}" }
    }
    date {
        match => [ "timestamp" , "dd/MMM/yyyy:HH:mm:ss Z" ]
    }
-- INSERT --                                                    1,3              Top
```

Check the configuration of `/opt/bitnami/logstash/bin/logstash -f`
`/opt/bitnami/logstash/conf/ --config.test_and_exit`:

Start Logstash as follows:

```
sudo /opt/bitnami/ctlscript.sh start logstash
```

Check if Elasticsearch is working well:

Now, let's go to Kibana. As you may have noticed, we don't have an index pattern yet:

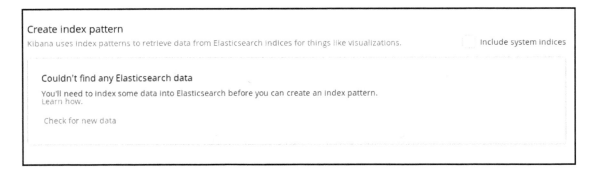

After configuring Logstash, we can create a new index pattern:

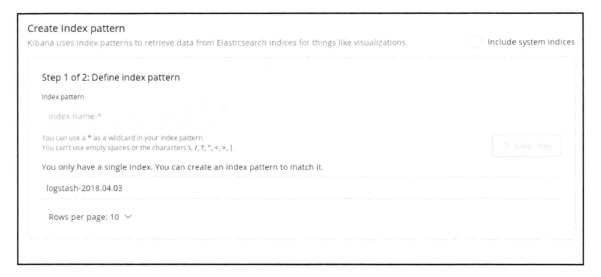

Type * and click **Next step**:

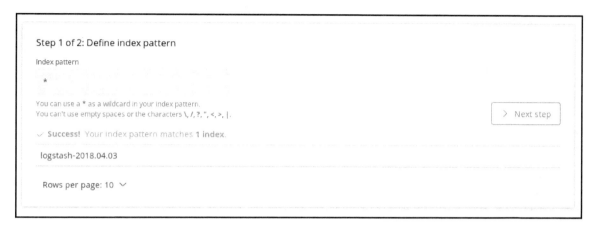

Select **@timestamp** and click the **Create Index pattern** button. You can now view the new index pattern page in Kibana:

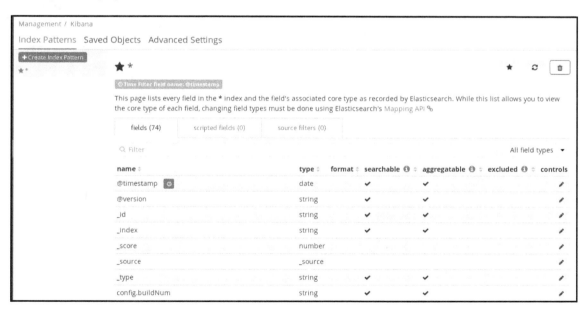

When you hit the **Discover** option, you can check the logs:

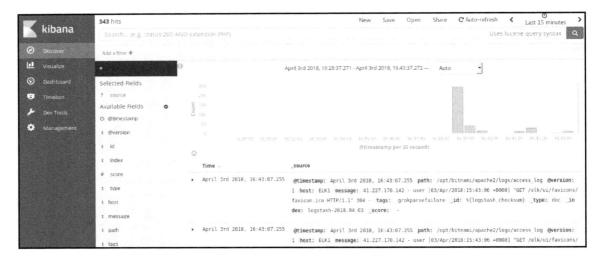

Now, let's customize a visualization to add to the main dashboard later. Click **Visualize** on the side list, and create a new visualization:

For our demonstration, we are going to use the **Vertical Bar**. You can choose from a range of charts and visualization tools:

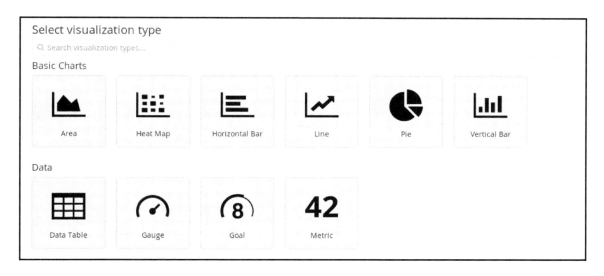

For the **X-Axis,** select **Date Histogram** as the **Aggregation** and **@timestamp** as the **Field**:

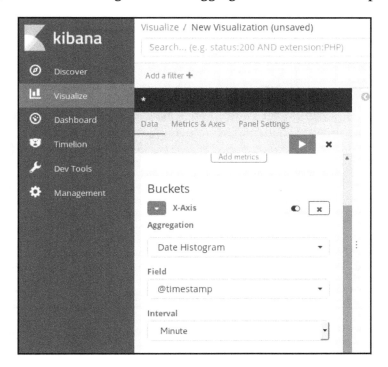

You will then see a visualization of your chart, as the following screenshot illustrates:

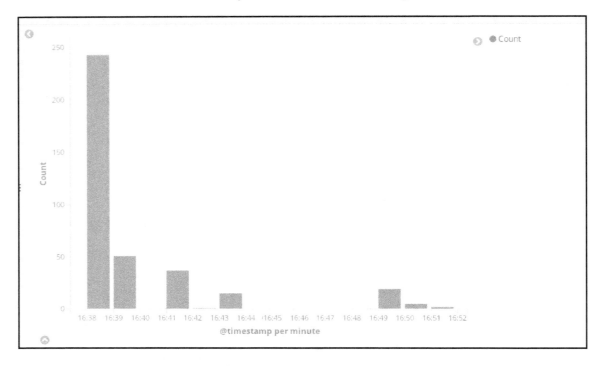

After creating the visualization, let's add to our dashboard. Click on the **Dashboard** link and create a new dashboard. Then, add your visualizations:

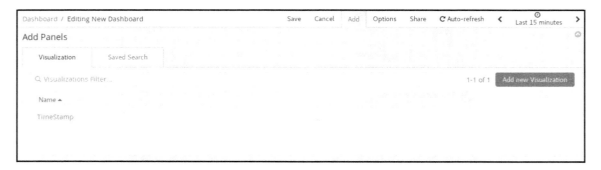

Save the dashboard. Now, you can check any indicator:

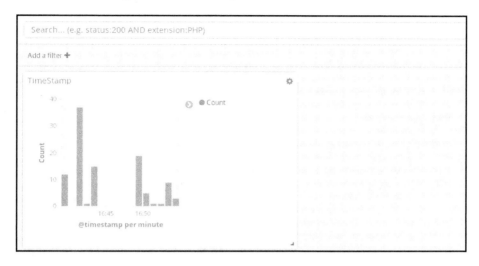

The ELK Stack threat platform is ready to help you hunt a number of advanced threats. Let's take our project up a notch and add an intelligent touch to it by using the power of machine learning to automate hunting operations. The ELK Stack gives you the power to add a plugin called X-Pack to your hunting platform, which will help you to detect anomalies in your artifacts and logs.

To get the X-Pack plugin, we need to install it on every layer of the stack, as this official illustration shows:

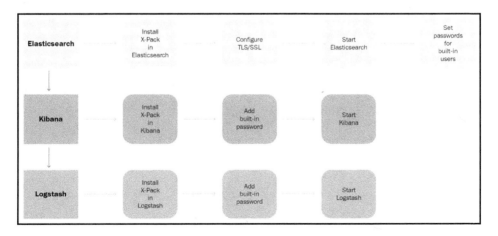

To install the plugin on Elasticsearch, go to the `binaries` folder and type in the following command:

```
./elasticsearch-plugin install x-pack
```

The same action applies to Kibana:

```
sudo bin/kibana-plugin install x-pack
```

It also applies to Logstash:

```
sudo bin/logstash-plugin install x-pack
```

Restart all of the services and go to the Kibana dashboard; you will notice a new option, called **Machine Learning**:

Finally, you can add a time series anomaly detection capability, thanks to X-Pack. In the previous chapter we discussed anomaly detection in a detailed way. We dived deep into anomaly detection fundamentals and how to use machine learning to detect those anomalies. X-Pack is using the same techniques to spot anomalies.

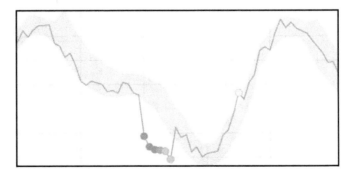

Summary

In previous chapters, we saw how to build anomaly detection systems from scratch by using different machine learning algorithms and Python libraries. This chapter included a step-by-step guide to help you build a fully functioning threat-hunting platform, using three amazing open source projects. We also implemented a machine learning plugin to optimize and enhance the threat-hunting platform's power. By now, you have learned how to build many defensive systems using the power of machine learning. The next chapter is a must-read if you want to learn how to bypass machine learning safeguards.

Questions

1. Which of the following is not a step in the cyber kill chain?

    (a) Scanning
    (b) Control and command
    (c) Discover and spread

2. Which of the following options is not a node of the diamond model of intrusion analysis?

    (a) Victims
    (b) Infrastructure
    (c) Procedures

3. How many parts are needed in a Logstash configuration file?

    (a) 2
    (b) 3
    (c) 4

4. In ElasticSearch, what is indexing?

    (a) The process of storing data in an index
    (b) The process of identifying data
    (c) None of the above

5. In Elasticsearch, what is a node?

    (a) An Elasticsearch module
    (b) An instance of Elasticsearch
    (c) None of the above

6. In Elasticsearch, what is a shard?

    (a) Shared files
    (b) Shared data
    (c) Shared resources (RAM, vCPU, and so on)

7. Does Elasticsearch have a schema? (Yes | No)

8
Evading Intrusion Detection Systems

Deploying intrusion detection systems is essential for every modern company, in order to defend against attackers. In the previous chapters, we learned how to build machine learning, based intrusion detection systems. Now, it is time to learn how to bypass these systems with adversarial learning; to defend your systems, you need to learn how to attack them first.

In this chapter, we will cover the following:

- Adversarial machine learning algorithms
- Machine learning threat models
- Evading intrusion detection systems with adversarial network systems

Technical requirements

In this chapter, you will need the following libraries:

- PyYAML
- NumPy
- SciPy
- CVXPY
- Python 3
- Matplotlib
- scikit-learn
- Progress
- Pathos

- CVXOPT (optional, as a CVXPY solver)
- Jupyter Notebook

You can find the code files at `https://github.com/PacktPublishing/Mastering-Machine-Learning-for-Penetration-Testing/tree/master/Chapter08`.

Adversarial machine learning algorithms

Before studying adversarial machine learning, let's explore two important terminologies: overfitting and underfitting.

Overfitting and underfitting

Overfitting is one of the biggest obstacles that machine learning practitioners face. Knowing how to spot overfitting is a required skill for building robust machine learning models, because achieving 99% accuracy is not the end of the story. In machine learning, we make predictions. By definition, the **fit** is how well we approximate the target function. As we saw in the first chapter, the aim of supervised learning is to map the function between the input data and the targets. Thus, a good fit is a good approximation of that function.

Overfitting happens when a model learns the details and noise in the training data, to the extent that it negatively impacts the performance of the model. In other words, noise is picked up and learned by the model, so it can no longer generalize well when it is fed new data. The following graph illustrates an overfitting situation. You will notice that the model has been trained too well, which makes it hard to achieve accuracy when we feed the model with data.

Another obstacle is underfitting. This occurs when a machine learning model does not fit the data well enough. In other words, when the model is too simple:

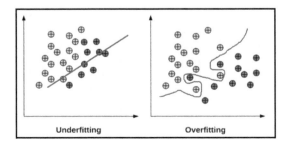

Overfitting and underfitting with Python

Let's look at a real-world demonstration of overfitting and underfitting, with scikit-learn. Import the required modules:

```
import numpy as np
import matplotlib.pyplot as plt
from sklearn.pipeline import Pipeline
from sklearn.preprocessing import PolynomialFeatures
from sklearn.linear_model import LinearRegression
from sklearn.model_selection import cross_val_score
```

We will now build a small model and visualize the model, the samples, and the `true` function, to see overfitting and underfitting. We will use the following code:

```
np.random.seed(0)
n_samples = 30
degrees = [1, 4, 15]
X = np.sort(np.random.rand(n_samples))
y = np.cos(1.5 * np.pi * X) + np.random.randn(n_samples) * 0.1
plt.figure(figsize=(14, 5))

for i in range(len(degrees)):
 ax = plt.subplot(1, len(degrees), i + 1)
  plt.setp(ax, xticks=(), yticks=())

polynomial_features = PolynomialFeatures(degree=degrees[i],
include_bias=False)
linear_regression = LinearRegression()
pipeline = Pipeline([("polynomial_features", polynomial_features),
("linear_regression", linear_regression)])
pipeline.fit(X[:, np.newaxis], y)

# Evaluate the models using crossvalidation
scores = cross_val_score(pipeline, X[:, np.newaxis], y,
scoring="neg_mean_squared_error", cv=10)

X_test = np.linspace(0, 1, 100)
 plt.plot(X_test, pipeline.predict(X_test[:, np.newaxis]), label="Model")
 plt.plot(X_test, true_fun(X_test), label="True function")
 plt.scatter(X, y, edgecolor='b', s=20, label="Samples")
 plt.xlabel("x")
 plt.ylabel("y")
 plt.xlim((0, 1))
 plt.ylim((-2, 2))
 plt.legend(loc="best")
 plt.title("Degree {}\nMSE = {:.2e}(+/- {:.2e})".format(
```

```
    degrees[i], -scores.mean(), scores.std()))
    plt.show()
```

By running the previous script, we draw the following graphs that illustrate 3 cases: under-fitting, Good fitting and over-fitting (from left to right):

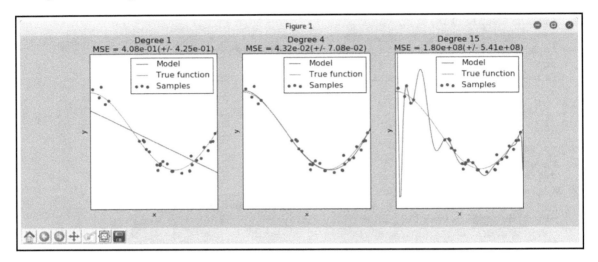

The following table was created using the terms highlighted in the previous code, and the corresponding URLs:

Modules	URL
plt.subplot	https://matplotlib.org/api/_as_gen/matplotlib.pyplot.subplot.html#matplotlib.pyplot.subplot
plt.setp	http://matplotlib.org/api/_as_gen/matplotlib.pyplot.setp.html#matplotlib.pyplot.setp
PolynomialFeatures	http://scikit-learn.org/stable/modules/generated/sklearn.preprocessing.PolynomialFeatures.html#sklearn.preprocessing.PolynomialFeatures
LinearRegression	http://scikit-learn.org/stable/modules/generated/sklearn.linear_model.LinearRegression.html#sklearn.linear_model.LinearRegression
Pipeline	http://scikit-learn.org/stable/modules/generated/sklearn.pipeline.Pipeline.html#sklearn.pipeline.Pipeline
np.newaxis	http://docs.scipy.org/doc/numpy-1.8.1/reference/arrays.indexing.html#numpy.newaxis

cross_val_score	http://scikit-learn.org/stable/modules/generated/sklearn. model_selection.cross_val_score.html#sklearn.model_ selection.cross_val_score
np.newaxis	http://docs.scipy.org/doc/numpy-1.8.1/reference/arrays. indexing.html#numpy.newaxis
np.linspace	http://docs.scipy.org/doc/numpy-1.8.1/reference/ generated/numpy.linspace.html#numpy.linspace
plt.plot	http://matplotlib.org/api/_as_gen/matplotlib.pyplot.plot. html#matplotlib.pyplot.plot
plt.scatter	http://matplotlib.org/api/_as_gen/matplotlib.pyplot. scatter.html#matplotlib.pyplot.scatter
plt.xlabel	http://matplotlib.org/api/_as_gen/matplotlib.pyplot. xlabel.html#matplotlib.pyplot.xlabel
plt.ylabel	http://matplotlib.org/api/_as_gen/matplotlib.pyplot. ylabel.html#matplotlib.pyplot.ylabel
plt.xlim	http://matplotlib.org/api/_as_gen/matplotlib.pyplot.xlim. html#matplotlib.pyplot.xlim
plt.ylim	http://matplotlib.org/api/_as_gen/matplotlib.pyplot.ylim. html#matplotlib.pyplot.ylim
plt.legend	http://matplotlib.org/api/legend_api.html#matplotlib. legend
plt.title	http://matplotlib.org/api/_as_gen/matplotlib.pyplot. title.html#matplotlib.pyplot.title
plt.show	http://matplotlib.org/api/_as_gen/matplotlib.pyplot.show. html#matplotlib.pyplot.show

Detecting overfitting

To detect overfitting, it is highly recommended to split the initial dataset into a training set and a testing set. If the training set performs way better than the testing set, then we have a problem. Also, it is highly recommended to start with a simple algorithm and move on to more complex models later, checking whether upgrading the level of complexity was worth it. To defend against overfitting, we can use cross-validation. Cross-validation is the process of evaluating many machine learning techniques by training models with different subsets (*k* subsets).

Adversarial machine learning

Adversarial machine learning is the art of studying how to break and secure machine learning models. You can consider it an intersection between machine learning and information security. As a security professional, learning how to build defensive layers with machine learning is important, but knowing how to break them is also an amazing addition to your skill set:

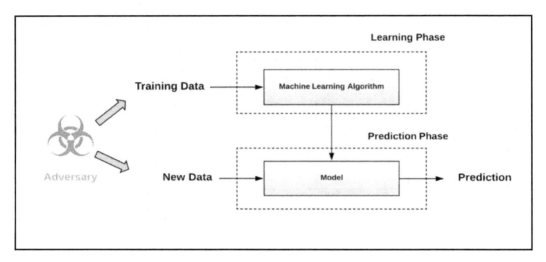

In 2006, Barreno, et al., proposed a taxonomy for the threat models against machine learning systems. The model is based on three axes:

- Influence
- Security violations
- Specificity

In 2011, the model was extended by Huang, et al., to include another axis, called **privacy**. In 2016, Papernot, McDaniel, Jha, Fredrikson, Celik, and Swami, introduced a new taxonomy that focuses on only two axes:

- Complexity of the attack
- Knowledge of the attacker

The following diagram illustrates the machine learning threat taxonomy:

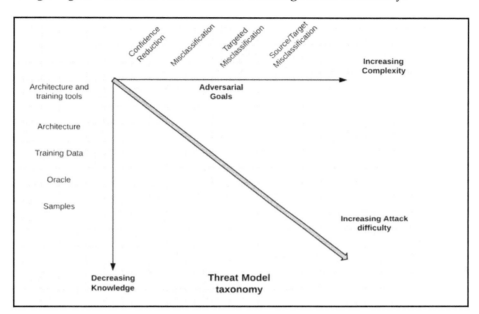

To attack machine learning models, attackers can perform many techniques, addressed in the following sections.

Evasion attacks

To perform machine learning evasion attacks, cyber criminals try to bypass the learning outcomes by observing how the model works, especially the outcome, by trying many different samples simply by feeding the model with different inputs and trying to find the learning patterns. This technique is very popular. For example, if an attacker wants to bypass a machine learning spam filter, he needs to feed the system with different emails and search for a pattern that makes a spam email goes through (Not detected as a spam email) and bypass detection by doing only a few modifications to previously detected emails.

The following workflow illustrates how an evasion attack works:

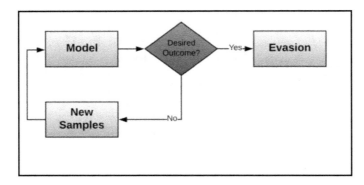

Poisoning attacks

In machine learning poisoning attacks, attackers poison the model in order to change the learning outcome, by adding malicious data in the model training phase. This method can be performed, for example, by sending and injecting carefully designed samples when data collection is occurring during network operations, to train a network intrusion detection system model. The following workflow illustrates how a poisoning attack occurs:

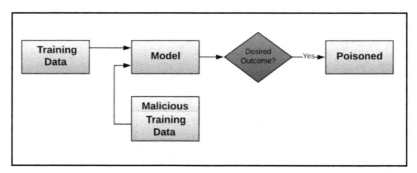

Some of the greatest research conducted on adversarial machine learning was done in the *Pattern recognition and applications lab Italy,* including *Poisoning Attacks Against Support Vector Machines,* when Battista Biggio and his team presented a great framework to attack support vector machine systems. The steps are as follows:

1. Identify a proper adversary's goal
2. Define the adversary's knowledge

3. Formulate the corresponding optimization problem
4. Resample the collected (training and test) data accordingly
5. Evaluate the classifier's security on the resampled data
6. Repeat the evaluation for different levels of adversary knowledge

 If you are familiar with MATLAB, I highly recommend that you to try **ALFASVMLib**. It is a MATLAB library on adversarial label flip attacks on SVM. You can download it from `https://github.com/feuerchop/ALFASVMLib`.

Adversarial clustering

Clustering techniques are widely used in many real-world applications. Attackers are coming up with new techniques to attack clustering models. One of them is adversarial clustering, wherein the attackers manipulate the input data (adding a small percentage of attack samples), so that the newly added sample can hide within the existing clusters.

Adversarial features

Feature selection is an important step in every machine learning project. Attackers are also using adversarial feature selection to attack models. I highly recommend that you read the research done by the same team (*Pattern recognition and applications lab Italy researchers*), presented in a paper called, *Is Feature Selection Secure Against Training Data Poisoning?*

The team showed that by poisoning the embedded feature selection algorithms, including LASSO, ridge regression, and the ElasticNet, they fooled a PDF malware detector.

There are many Python frameworks and open source projects that were developed by researchers to attack and evaluate machine learning models, like **CleverHans**, the **Adversarial Machine Learning** (AML) library, and **EvadeML-Zoo**.

CleverHans

CleverHans is under continual development; it is an adversarial example library for constructing attacks, building defenses, and benchmarking machine learning systems' vulnerability to adversarial attacks.

You can clone it from `https://github.com/tensorflow/cleverhans`:

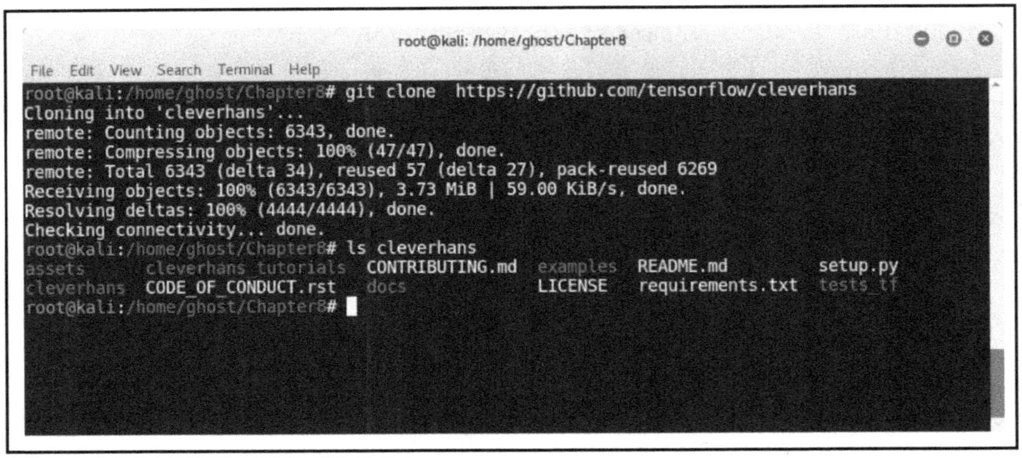

Or, you can install it by using the `pip` utility, as shown here:

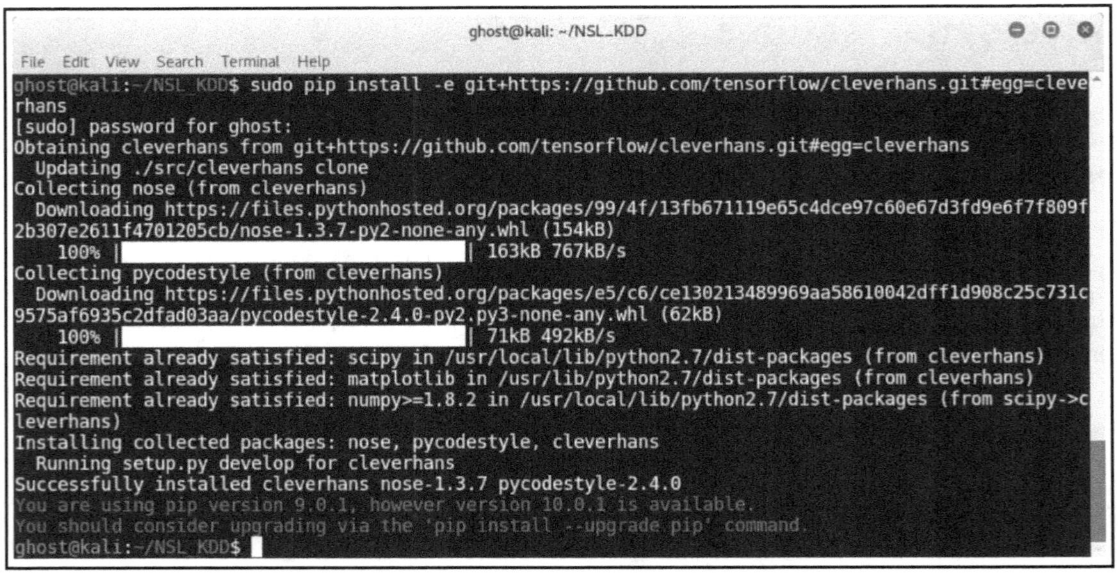

The AML library

The AML library is a game-theoretic adversarial machine learning library, developed by the Computational Economics Research Lab at Vanderbilt University. By game theory we mean the study of mathematical models of cooperation between intelligent decision making agents. You can clone the library from `https://github.com/vu-aml/adlib`.

EvadeML-Zoo

EvadeML-Zoo is a benchmarking and visualization tool for adversarial machine learning, developed by the Machine Learning Group and the Security Research Group at the University of Virginia. You can download it from `https://github.com/mzweilin/EvadeML-Zoo`.

Evading intrusion detection systems with adversarial network systems

By now, you will have acquired a fair understanding of adversarial machine learning, and how to attack machine learning models. It's time to dive deep into more technical details, learning how to bypass machine learning based intrusion detection systems with Python. You will also learn how to defend against those attacks.

In this demonstration, you are going to learn how to attack the model with a poisoning attack. As discussed previously, we are going to inject malicious data, so that we can influence the learning outcome of the model. The following diagram illustrates how the poisoning attack will occur:

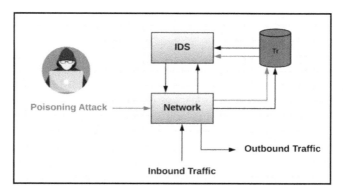

In this attack, we are going to use a **Jacobian-Based Saliency Map Attack (JSMA)**. This is done by searching for adversarial examples by modifying only a limited number of pixels in an input.

Let's look at how to attack a machine based intrusion detection system with Python. The code is a little bit long, so I am only going to include some important snippets; later, you can find the full code in the chapter's GitHub repository.

For this project, we need the NumPy, pandas, Keras, CleverHans, TensorFlow, scikit-learn, and matplotlib Python libraries.

These are some of the imported libraries:

```
import numpy as np
import pandas as pd
from keras.models import Sequential
from keras.layers import Dense , Dropout
from keras.optimizers import RMSprop , adam
from cleverhans.attacks import fgsm , jsma
from cleverhans.utils_tf import model_train , model_eval , batch_eval
from cleverhans.attacks_tf import jacobian_graph
from cleverhans.utils import other_classes
import tensorflow as tf
from sklearn.tree import DecisionTreeClassifier
from sklearn.ensemble import RandomForestClassifier
from sklearn.linear_model import LogisticRegression
from sklearn.metrics import accuracy_score , roc_curve , auc , f1_score
from sklearn.preprocessing import LabelEncoder , MinMaxScaler
import matplotlib.pyplot as plt
```

The next step is pre-processing the data:

```
names = ['duration', 'protocol', 'service ', 'flag', 'src_bytes',
'dst_bytes', 'land',
'wrong_fragment ','urgent ', 'hot', 'num_failed_logins ', 'logged_in ',
'num_compromised ', 'root_shell ', 'su_attempted ','num_root ',
'num_file_creations ', 'num_shells ', 'num_access_files ',
'num_outbound_cmds ','is_host_login ', 'is_guest_login ', 'count',
'srv_count ', 'serror_rate', 'srv_serror_rate ','rerror_rate ',
'srv_rerror_rate ', 'same_srv_rate ', 'diff_srv_rate', 'srv_diff_host_rate
','dst_host_count ', 'dst_host_srv_count ', 'dst_host_same_srv_rate ',
'dst_host_diff_srv_rate ','dst_host_same_src_port_rate ',
'dst_host_srv_diff_host_rate ', 'dst_host_serror_rate
','dst_host_srv_serror_rate ','dst_host_rerror_rate ',
'dst_host_srv_rerror_rate ','attack_type ', 'other ']
```

We will then load the data with pandas:

```
TrainingData = pd.read_csv('KDDTrain+.txt', names=names , header=None)
TestingData = pd.read_csv('KDDTest+.txt', names=names , header=None)
```

Then, concatenate the training and testing sets:

```
All = pd.concat ([TrainingData, TestingData])
assert full.shape[0] == TrainingData.shape[0] + TestingData.shape[0]
```

Select the data and identify the features:

```
All['label'] = full['attack_type']
```

To identify DoS attacks, use the following:

```
All.loc[All.label == 'neptune ', 'label'] = 'dos'
All.loc[All.label == 'back', 'label '] = 'dos'
All.loc[All.label == 'land', 'label '] = 'dos'
All.loc[All.label == 'pod', 'label'] = 'dos'
All.loc[All.label == 'smurf ', 'label'] = 'dos'
All.loc[All.label == 'teardrop ', 'label '] = 'dos'
All.loc[All.label == 'mailbomb ', 'label '] = 'dos'
All.loc[All.label == 'processtable ', 'label'] = 'dos'
All.loc[All.label == 'udpstorm ', 'label '] = 'dos'
All.loc[All.label == 'apache2 ', 'label'] = 'dos'
All.loc[All.label == 'worm', 'label '] = 'dos'
```

Identify other attacks (**User-to-Root (U2R)**, **Remote-to -Local (R2L)**, and **Probe**) with the same technique.

To generate one-hot encoding, use the following:

```
full = pd.get_dummies(All , drop_first=False)
```

Identify the training and testing sets again:

```
features = list(full.columns [:-5])
y_train = np.array(full[0:TrainingData.shape[0]][[ 'label_normal ',
'label_dos ', 'label_probe
label_r2l ', 'label_u2r ']])
X_train = full[0:TrainingData.shape[0]][ features]
y_test = np.array(full[TrainingData.shape[0]:][[ 'label_normal ',
'label_dos ', 'label_probe ', '
label_r2l ', 'label_u2r ']])
X_test = full[TrainingData.shape[0]:][features]
```

To scale the data, use the following command:

```
scaler = MinMaxScaler().fit(X_train)
```

An example of `scale X_train` is as follows:

```
X_train_scaled = np.array(scaler.transform(X_train))
```

Let's suppose that we are going to attack a logistic regression model; we need to process data to train that model and generate label encoding:

```
labels = All.label.unique()
En = LabelEncoder()
En.fit(labels)
y_All = En.transform(All.label)
y_train_l = y_All[0:TrainingData.shape[0]]
y_test_l = y_All[TrainingData.shape[0]:]
```

We have now completed the pre-processing phase.

For the Jacobian-Based Saliency Map attack, we are going to use the following Python implementation:

```
results = np.zeros((FLAGS.nb_classes , source_samples), dtype='i')
perturbations = np.zeros((FLAGS.nb_classes , source_samples), dtype='f')
grads = jacobian_graph(predictions , x, FLAGS.nb_classes)
X_adv = np.zeros(( source_samples , X_test_scaled.shape [1]))
for sample_ind in range(0, source_samples):
current_class = int(np.argmax(y_test[sample_ind ]))
for target in [0]:
if current_class == 0:
Break
adv_x , res , percent_perturb = jsma(sess , x, predictions ,
grads,X_test_scaled[sample_ind: (sample_ind+1)],target , theta=1, gamma
=0.1,increase=True , back='tf',clip_min=0, clip_max =1)
X_adv[sample_ind] = adv_x
results[target , sample_ind] = res
perturbations[target , sample_ind] = percent_perturb
```

To build a `MultiLayer Perceptron` network, use the following code snippet:

```
def mlp_model ():
    Generate a MultiLayer Perceptron model
    model = Sequential ()
    model.add(Dense (256, activation='relu', input_shape =(
X_train_scaled.shape [1],)))
    model.add(Dropout (0.4))
    model.add(Dense (256, activation='relu'))
```

```
model.add(Dropout (0.4))
model.add(Dense(FLAGS.nb_classes , activation='softmax
'))model.compile(loss='categorical_crossentropy ',optimizer='adam',metrics
=['accuracy '])
model.summary ()
return model
```

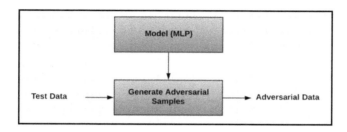

For adversarial prediction, use the following:

```
y_pred_adv = dt.predict(X_adv)
fpr_dt_adv , tpr_dt_adv , _ = roc_curve(y_test[:, 0], y_pred_adv [:, 0])
roc_auc_dt_adv = auc(fpr_dt_adv , tpr_dt_adv)
print("Accuracy score adversarial:", accuracy_score(y_test , y_pred_adv))
print("F1 score adversarial:", f1_score(y_test , y_pred_adv ,
average='micro '))
print("AUC score adversarial:", roc_auc_dt_adv)
```

Finally, we need to evaluate the model by feeding it with the adversarial testing data:

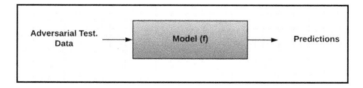

 If you get errors, check the chapter's GitHub repository. The code may be updated and enhanced after publishing this book.

Summary

In this chapter, we provided an overview of adversarial learning techniques, and described how attackers and cyber criminals perform attacks against machine learning models.

The next chapter will be a great complementary guide, exploring how to attack artificial neural networks and deep learning networks. You will learn how attackers can bypass modern anti-malware systems by using adversarial deep learning and reinforcement learning.

Questions

1. Can you briefly explain why overtraining a machine learning model is not a good idea?
2. What is the difference between overfitting and underfitting?
3. What is the difference between an evasion and poisoning attack?
4. How does adversarial clustering work?
5. What type of adversarial attack is used to avoid the intrusion detection system?
6. Is the preceding attack an evasion or poisoning attack?

Further reading

- *The Malicious Use of Artificial Intelligence: Forecasting, Prevention, and Mitigation*: https://img1.wsimg.com/blobby/go/3d82daa4-97fe-4096-9c6b-376b92c619de/downloads/1c6q2kc4v_50335.pdf
- *Attacking Machine Learning with Adversarial Examples*: https://blog.openai.com/adversarial-example-research/
- *Awesome Adversarial Machine Learning*: https://github.com/yenchenlin/awesome-adversarial-machine-learning
- *Ensemble Adversarial Training: Attacks and Defenses*: https://arxiv.org/pdf/1705.07204.pdf
- *Introduction to Adversarial Machine Learning*: https://mascherari.press/introduction-to-adversarial-machine-learning/
- *Adversarial Deep Learning Against Intrusion Detection Classifiers*: http://www.diva-portal.org/smash/get/diva2:1116037/FULLTEXT01.pdf

- *Is Feature Selection Secure Against Training Data Poisoning?* (`http://pralab.diee.unica.it/sites/default/files/biggio15-icml.pdf`)
- *Security evaluation of learning algorithms*: `http://pralab.diee.unica.it/en/SecurityEvaluation`
- *General Framework for AI and Security Threats*: `https://img1.wsimg.com/blobby/go/3d82daa4-97fe-4096-9c6b-376b92c619de/downloads/1c6q2kc4v_50335.pdf`
- *The challenge of verification and testing of machine learning*: `http://www.cleverhans.io/security/privacy/ml/2017/06/14/verification.html`:
- *Attacks Against Intrusion Detection Networks: Evasion, Reverse Engineering, and Optimal Countermeasures* (PhD thesis): `http://www.seg.inf.uc3m.es/~spastran/phd/PhD_Thesis_Sergio_Pastrana.pdf`

9

Bypassing Machine Learning Malware Detectors

In the previous chapter, you learned that you can break into machine learning models and make them perform malicious activities by using adversarial machine learning techniques. In this chapter, we are going to explore further techniques, like how to fool artificial neural networks and deep learning networks. We are going to look at anti-malware system evasion as a case study.

In this chapter, we will cover the following:

- Adversarial deep learning
- How to bypass next generation malware detectors with generative adversarial networks
- Bypassing machine learning with reinforcement learning

Technical requirements

You can find the code files for this chapter at `https://github.com/PacktPublishing/Mastering-Machine-Learning-for-Penetration-Testing/tree/master/Chapter09`.

Adversarial deep learning

Information security professionals are doing their best to come up with novel techniques to detect malware and malicious software. One of the trending techniques is using the power of machine learning algorithms to detect malware. On the other hand, attackers and cyber criminals are also coming up with new approaches to bypass next-generation systems. In the previous chapter, we looked at how to attack machine learning models and how to bypass intrusion detection systems.

Malware developers use many techniques to bypass machine learning malware detectors. Previously, we explored an approach to build malware classifiers by training the system with grayscale image vectors. In a demonstration done by the **Search And RetrieVAl of Malware (SARVAM)** research unit, at the Vision Research Lab, UCSB, the researchers illustrated that, by changing a few bytes, a model can classify a malware as a goodware. This technique can be performed by attackers to bypass malware classifiers, through changing a few bytes and pixels. In the demonstration, the researchers used a variant of the NETSTAT program, which is a command-line network utility tool that displays network connections. In the following image, the left-hand side is a representation of the NETSTAT.EXE malware, and the second is detected as a goodware. As you can see, the difference between the two programs is unnoticeable (88 bytes out of 36,864 bytes: 0.78%), after converting the two types of files into grayscale images and checking the differences between the two of them:

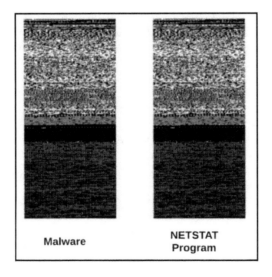

This technique is just the beginning; in this chapter, we are going to dive deep into how we can trick them (the machine learning model, in our case the malware classifier) into performing malicious activities.

The previous chapter was an overview of adversarial machine learning. We learned how machine learning can be bypassed by attackers. In this chapter, we are going to go deeper, discovering how to bypass malware machine learning based detectors; before that, we are going to learn how to fool artificial neural networks and avoid deep learning networks with Python, open source libraries, and open source projects. Neural networks can be tricked by **adversarial samples**. Adversarial samples are used as inputs to the neural network, to influence the learning outcome. A pioneering research project, called *Explaining and Harnessing Adversarial Networks,* conducted by Ian J. Goodfellow, Jonathon Shlens, and Christian Szegedy (at Google), showed that a small amount of carefully constructed noise can fool the neural network into thinking that the entered image is an image of a gibbon and not a panda, with 99.3% confidence. The neural network originally thought that the provided image was a panda, with 57.7% confidence, which is true; but it is not the case in the second example, after fooling the network:

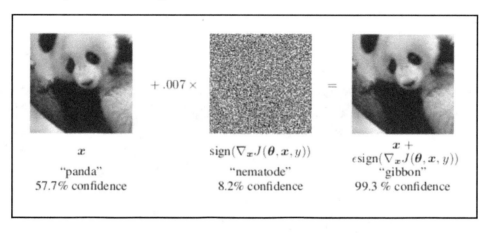

Many electronic devices and systems rely on deep learning as a protection mechanism, including face recognition; imagine what attackers can do to attack them and gain unauthorized access to critical systems.

Now, let's try to fool a neural network. We are going to fool a handwritten digit detector system by using the famous MNIST dataset. In `Chapter 4`, *Malware Detection with Deep Learning*, we learned how to build one. For the demonstration, we are going to fool a pretrained neural network by Michael Nielsen. He used 50,000 training images and 10,000 test images. Or, you can simply use your own neural network. You can find the training information in the GitHub repository of this chapter. The file is called `trained_network.pkl`; you will also find the MNIST file (`mnist.pkl.gz`):

```
import network.network as network
import network.mnist_loader as mnist_loader
```

```
# To serialize data
import pickle
import matplotlib.pyplot as plt
import numpy as np
```

Let's check whether the model is well-trained. Load the `pickle` file. Load the data with `pickle.load()`, and identify training,validation, and testing data:

```
Model = pickle.load( open( "trained_network.pkl", "rb" ) )    trainData,
valData, testData =mnist_loader.load_data_wrapper()
```

To check digit **2**, for example, we are going to select `test_data[1][0]`:

```
>>> data = test_data[1][0]
>>> activations = Model.feedforward(data)
>>> prediction = np.argmax(activations)
```

The following screenshot illustrates the preceding code:

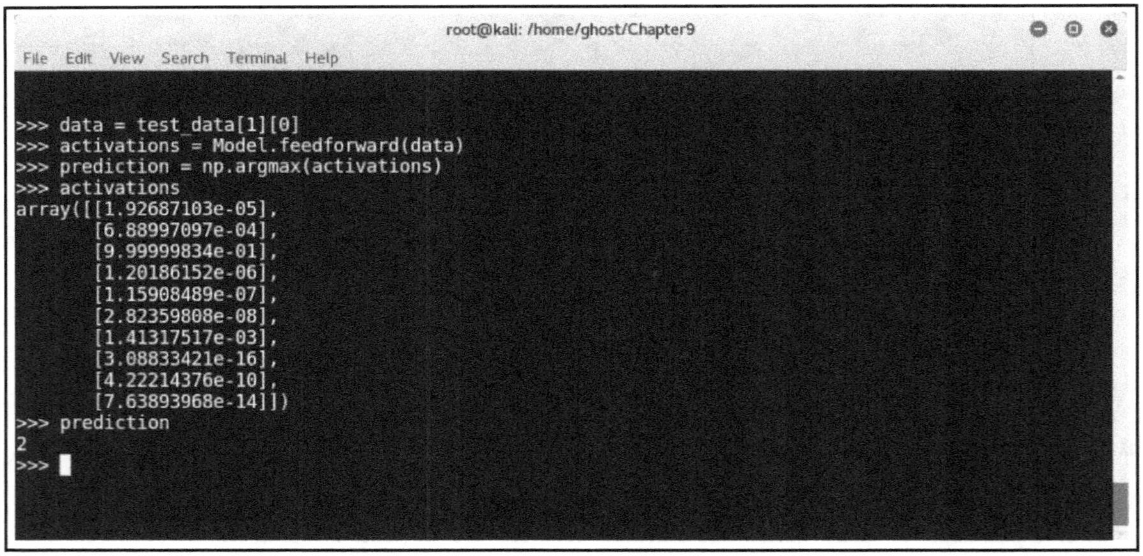

Plot the result to check further by using `matplotlib.pyplot (plt)`:

```
>>> plt.imshow(data.reshape((28,28)), cmap='Greys')
>>> plt.show()
```

As you can see we generated the digit **2** so the model was trained well:

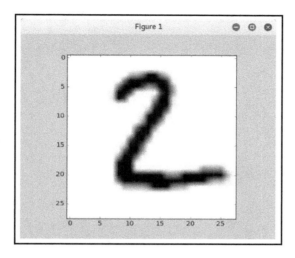

Everything is set up correctly. Now, we are going to attack the neural network with two types of attacks: **targeted** and **non-targeted.**

For a non-targeted attack, we are going to generate an adversarial sample and make the network give a certain output, for example, *6*:

$$Y = \begin{bmatrix} 0 \\ 0 \\ 0 \\ 0 \\ 0 \\ 0 \\ 1 \\ 0 \\ 0 \\ 0 \end{bmatrix}$$

In this attack, we want the neural network to think that the image entered is *6*. The target image (let's call it *X)* is a *784* dimensional vector, because the image dimension is *28×28* pixels. Our goal is to find a vector $\bar{x}$ that minimizes the cost *C*, resulting in an image that the neural network predicts as our goal label. The cost function, *C*, is defined as the following:

$$C = \frac{1}{2} \times \|Y_{goal} - \hat{y}(\vec{x})\|_2^2$$

The following code block is an implementation of a derivative function:

```
def input_derivative(net, x, y):
    """ Calculate derivatives wrt the inputs"""
    nabla_b = [np.zeros(b.shape) for b in net.biases]
    nabla_w = [np.zeros(w.shape) for w in net.weights]
    # feedforward
    activation = x
    activations = [x] # list to store all the activations, layer by layer
    zs = [] # list to store all the z vectors, layer by layer
    for b, w in zip(net.biases, net.weights):
        z = np.dot(w, activation)+b
        zs.append(z)
        activation = sigmoid(z)
        activations.append(activation)
    # backward pass
    delta = net.cost_derivative(activations[-1], y) * \
        sigmoid_prime(zs[-1])
    nabla_b[-1] = delta
    nabla_w[-1] = np.dot(delta, activations[-2].transpose())

    for l in xrange(2, net.num_layers):
        z = zs[-l]
        sp = sigmoid_prime(z)
        delta = np.dot(net.weights[-l+1].transpose(), delta) * sp
        nabla_b[-l] = delta
        nabla_w[-l] = np.dot(delta, activations[-l-1].transpose())
    return net.weights[0].T.dot(delta)
```

To generate the adversarial sample, we need to set the goal:

```
goal = np.zeros((10, 1))
goal[n] = 1
```

Create a random image for gradient descent initialization, as follows:

```
x = np.random.normal(.5, .3, (784, 1))
```

Compute the gradient descent, as follows:

```
for i in range(steps):
        # Calculate the derivative
        d = input_derivative(net,x,goal)
        x -= eta * d
    return x
```

Now, you can generate the sample:

```
a = adversarial(net, n, 1000, 1)
x = np.round(net.feedforward(a), 2)
Print ("The input is:", str(x))
Print ("The prediction is", str(np.argmax(x)))
```

Plot the adversarial sample, as follows:

```
plt.imshow(a.reshape(28,28), cmap='Greys')
plt.show()
```

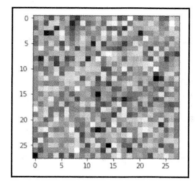

In targeted attacks, we use the same technique and the same code, but we add a new term to the cost function. So, it will be as follows:

$$C = \frac{1}{2} \times \|Y_{goal} - \hat{y}(\vec{x})\|_2^2 + \lambda \|\vec{x} - X_{target}\|_2^2$$

Foolbox

Foolbox is a Python toolbox to benchmark the robustness of machine learning models. It is supported by many frameworks, including the following:

- TensorFlow
- PyTorch
- Theano
- Keras
- Lasagne
- MXNet

To install Foolbox, use the `pip` utility:

```
pip install foolbox
```

The following are some Foolbox attacks:

- **Gradient-Based Attacks**: By linearizing the loss around an input, x
- **Gradient Sign Attack (FGSM)**: By computing the gradient, $g(x0)$, once, and then seeking the minimum step size
- **Iterative Gradient Attack**: By maximizing the loss along small steps in the gradient direction, $g(x)$
- **Iterative Gradient Sign Attack**: By maximizing the loss along small steps in the ascent direction, $sign(g(x))$
- **DeepFool L2Attack**: By computing, for each class, the minimum distance, $d(\ell, \ell0)$, that it takes to reach the class boundary
- **DeepFool L∞Attack**: Like L2Attack, but minimizes the *L∞-norm* instead
- **Jacobian-Based Saliency Map Attack**: By computing a saliency score for each input feature
- **Single Pixel Attack**: By setting a single pixel to white or black

To implement an attack with Foolbox, use the following:

```
import foolbox
import keras
import numpy as np
from keras.applications.resnet50 import ResNet50

keras.backend.set_learning_phase(0)
kmodel = ResNet50(weights='imagenet')
preprocessing = (np.array([104, 116, 123]), 1)
fmodel = foolbox.models.KerasModel(kmodel, bounds=(0, 255),
preprocessing=preprocessing)

image, label = foolbox.utils.imagenet_example()
attack = foolbox.attacks.FGSM(fmodel)
adversarial = attack(image[:, :, ::-1], label)
```

If you receive the error, `ImportError(``load_weights` requires h5py.')`, solve it by installing the **h5py** library (`pip install h5py`).

To plot the result, use the following code:

```
import matplotlib.pyplot as plt
plt.figure()
plt.subplot(1, 3, 1)
plt.title('Original')
plt.imshow(image / 255)
plt.axis('off')
plt.subplot(1, 3, 2)
plt.title('Adversarial')
plt.imshow(adversarial[:, :, ::-1] / 255)  # ::-1 to convert BGR to RGB
plt.axis('off')
plt.subplot(1, 3, 3)
plt.title('Difference')
difference = adversarial[:, :, ::-1] - image
plt.imshow(difference / abs(difference).max() * 0.2 + 0.5)
plt.axis('off')
plt.show()
```

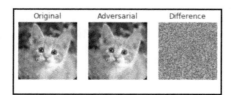

Deep-pwning

Deep-pwning is a lightweight framework for experimenting with machine learning models, with the goal of evaluating their robustness against a motivated adversary. It is called the **metasploit of machine learning**. You can clone it from the GitHub repository at `https://github.com/cchio/deep-pwning`.

Don't forget to install all of the requirements:

```
pip install -r requirements.txt
```

The following are the Python libraries required to work with Deep-pwning:

- Tensorflow 0.8.0
- Matplotlib >= 1.5.1
- Numpy >= 1.11.1
- Pandas >= 0.18.1
- Six >= 1.10.0

EvadeML

EvadeML (`https://evademl.org`) is an evolutionary framework based on genetic programming, for automatically finding variants that evade detection by machine learning based malware classifiers. It was developed by the Machine Learning Group and the Security Research Group at the University of Virginia.

To download EvadeML, clone it from `https://github.com/uvasrg/EvadeML`.

To install EvadeML, you need to install these required tools:

- A modified version of pdfrw for parsing PDFs: `https://github.com/mzweilin/pdfrw`
- Cuckoo Sandbox v1.2, as the oracle: `https://github.com/cuckoosandbox/cuckoo/releases/tag/1.2`
- The target classifier PDFrate-Mimicus: `https://github.com/srndic/mimicus`
- The target classifier Hidost: `https://github.com/srndic/hidost`

To configure the project, copy the template, and configure it with an editor:

```
cp project.conf.template project.conf
Vi  project.conf
```

Before running the main program, `./gp.py`, run the centralized detection agent with predefined malware signatures, as indicated in the documentation:

```
./utils/detection_agent_server.py ./utils/36vms_sigs.pickle
```

Select several benign PDF files:

```
./utils/generate_ext_genome.py [classifier_name] [benign_sample_folder]
[file_number]
```

To add a new classifier to evade, just add a wrapper in `./classifiers/`.

Bypassing next generation malware detectors with generative adversarial networks

In 2014, Ian Goodfellow, Yoshua Bengio, and their team, proposed a framework called the **generative adversarial network (GAN)**. Generative adversarial networks have the ability to generate images from a random noise. For example, we can train a generative network to generate images for handwritten digits from the MNIST dataset.

Generative adversarial networks are composed of two major parts: a **generator** and a **discriminator**.

The generator

The generator takes latent samples as inputs; they are randomly generated numbers, and they are trained to generate images:

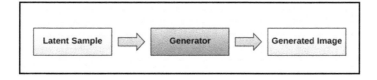

For example, to generate a handwritten digit, the generator will be a fully connected network that takes latent samples and generates 784 data points, reshaping them into *28x28* pixel images (MNIST digits). It is highly recommended to use `tanh` as an activation function:

```
generator = Sequential([
Dense(128, input_shape=(100,)),
LeakyReLU(alpha=0.01),
Dense(784),
Activation('tanh')
], name='generator')
```

The discriminator

The discriminator is simply a classifier trained with supervised learning techniques to check if the image is real (1) or fake (0). It is trained by both the MNIST dataset and the generator samples. The discriminator will classify the MNIST data as real, and the generator samples as fake:

```
discriminator = Sequential([
Dense(128, input_shape=(784,)),
LeakyReLU(alpha=0.01),
Dense(1),
Activation('sigmoid')], name='discriminator')
```

By connecting the two networks, the generator and the discriminator, we produce a generative adversarial network:

```
gan = Sequential([
generator,
discriminator])
```

This is a high-level representation of a generative adversarial network:

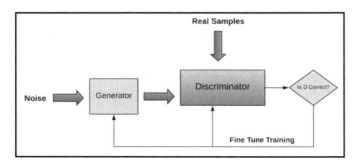

To train the GAN, we need to train the generator (the discriminator is set as non-trainable in further steps); in the training, the back-propagation updates the generator's weights to produce realistic images. So, to train a GAN, we use the following steps as a loop:

- Train the discriminator with the real images (the discriminator is trainable here)
- Set the discriminator as non-trainable
- Train the generator

The training loop will occur until both of the networks cannot be improved any further.

To build a GAN with Python, use the following code:

```python
import pickle as pkl
import numpy as np
import tensorflow as tf
import matplotlib.pyplot as plt
batch_size = 100
epochs = 100
samples = []
losses = []
saver = tf.train.Saver(var_list=g_vars)
with tf.Session() as sess:
    sess.run(tf.global_variables_initializer())
    for e in range(epochs):
        for ii in range(mnist.train.num_examples//batch_size):
            batch = mnist.train.next_batch(batch_size)
            batch_images = batch[0].reshape((batch_size, 784))
            batch_images = batch_images*2 - 1

            batch_z = np.random.uniform(-1, 1, size=(batch_size, z_size))
            _ = sess.run(d_train_opt, feed_dict={input_real: batch_images,
input_z: batch_z})
            _ = sess.run(g_train_opt, feed_dict={input_z: batch_z})
        train_loss_d = sess.run(d_loss, {input_z: batch_z, input_real:
batch_images})
        train_loss_g = g_loss.eval({input_z: batch_z})
        print("Epoch {}/{}...".format(e+1, epochs),
            "Discriminator Loss: {:.4f}...".format(train_loss_d),
            "Generator Loss: {:.4f}".format(train_loss_g))
        losses.append((train_loss_d, train_loss_g))
        sample_z = np.random.uniform(-1, 1, size=(16, z_size))
        gen_samples = sess.run(
                    generator(input_z, input_size,
n_units=g_hidden_size, reuse=True, alpha=alpha),
                    feed_dict={input_z: sample_z})
        samples.append(gen_samples)
```

```
        saver.save(sess, './checkpoints/generator.ckpt')
with open('train_samples.pkl', 'wb') as f:
    pkl.dump(samples, f)
```

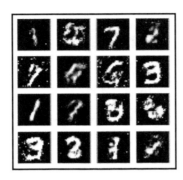

To build a GAN with Python, we are going to use NumPy and TensorFlow.

MalGAN

To generate malware samples to attack machine learning models, attackers are now using GANs to achieve their goals. Using the same techniques we discussed previously (a generator and a discriminator), cyber criminals perform attacks against next-generation anti-malware systems, even without knowing the machine learning technique used (black box attacks). One of these techniques is MalGAN, which was presented in a research project called, *Generating Adversarial Malware Examples for Black Box Attacks Based on GAN*, conducted by Weiwei Hu and Ying Tan from the Key Laboratory of Machine Perception (MOE) and the Department of Machine Intelligence. The architecture of MalGAN is as follows:

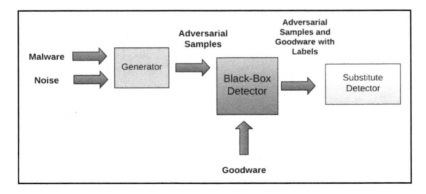

The generator creates adversarial malware samples by taking malware (feature vector *m*) and a noise vector, *z*, as input. The substitute detector is a multilayer, feed-forward neural network, which takes a program feature vector, *X*, as input. It classifies the program between a benign program and malware.

To train the generative adversarial network, the researchers used this algorithm:

```
While not converging do:
    Sample a minibatch of Malware M
    Generate adversarial samples M' from the generator
    Sample a minibatch of Goodware B
    Label M' and B using the detector
    Update the weight of the detector
    Update the generator weights
End while
```

Many of the samples generated may not be valid PE files. To preserve mutations and formats, the systems required a sandbox to ensure that functionality was preserved.

Generative adversarial network training cannot simply produce great results; that is why many hacks are needed to achieve better results. Some tricks were introduced by Soumith Chintala, Emily Denton, Martin Arjovsky, and Michael Mathieu, to obtain improved results:

- Normalizing the images between *-1* and *1*
- Using a max log, *D*, as a loss function, to optimize *G* instead of min (*log 1-D*)
- Sampling from a Gaussian distribution, instead of a uniform distribution
- Constructing different mini-batches for real and fake
- Avoiding ReLU and MaxPool, and using LeakyReLU and Average Pooling instead
- Using **Deep Convolutional GAN** (**DCGAN**), if possible
- Using the ADAM optimizer

Bypassing machine learning with reinforcement learning

In the previous technique, we noticed that if we are generating adversarial samples, especially if the outcomes are binaries, we will face some issues, including generating invalid samples. Information security researchers have come up with a new technique to bypass machine learning anti-malware systems with reinforcement learning.

Reinforcement learning

Previously (especially in the first chapter), we explored the different machine learning models: supervised, semi-supervised, unsupervised, and reinforcement models. Reinforcement machine learning models are important approaches to building intelligent machines. In reinforcement learning, an agent learns through experience, by interacting with an environment; it chooses the best decision based on a state and a reward function:

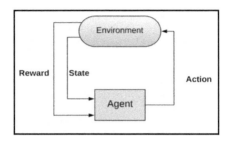

A famous example of reinforcement learning is the AI-based Atari Breakout. In this case, the environment includes the following:

- The ball and the bricks
- The moving paddle (left or right)
- The reward for eliminating the bricks

The following figure illustrates a high overview of the reinforcement model used to teach the model how to play Atari Breakout:

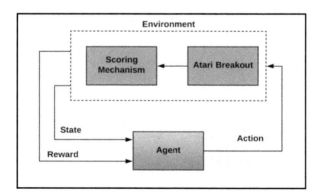

With the Atari Breakout environment as an analogy to learn how to avoid anti-malware systems, our environment will be as follows:

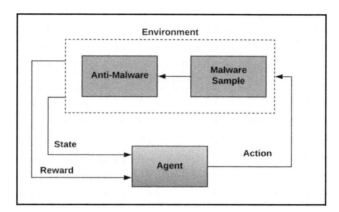

For the agent, it takes the environment state (general file information, header information, imported and exported functions, strings, and so on) to optimize its performance and the reward input from the antivirus reports, and result actions (creating entry points and new sections, modifying sections and so on). In other words, to perform and learn the agent is taking two inputs (States and rewards).

As an implementation of the concepts we've discussed, information security professionals worked on an OpenAI environment, to build a malware that can escape detection using reinforcement learning techniques. One of these environments is **Gym-malware**. This great environment was developed by endgame.

OpenAI gym contains an open source Python framework, developed by a nonprofit AI research company called OpenAI (https://openai.com/) to develop and evaluate reinforcement learning algorithms. To install OpenAI Gym, use the following code (you'll need to have Python 3.5+ installed):

```
git clone https://github.com/openai/gym
cd gym
pip install -e
```

OpenAI Gym is loaded pre-made environments. You can check all of the available environments at http://gym.openai.com/envs/:

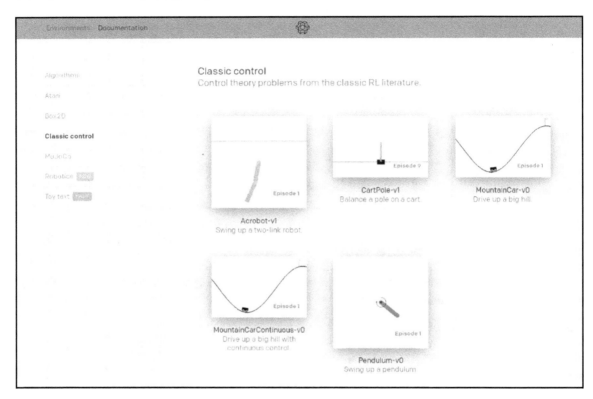

To run an environment with Python, you can use the following code; in this snippet, I chose the CartPole-v0 environment:

```
import gym
env = gym.make('CartPole-v0')
env.reset()
for _ in range(1000): # run for 1000 steps
    env.render()
    action = env.action_space.sampe() # pick a random action
    env.step(action) # take action
```

To use the Gym-malware environment, you will need to install Python 3.6 and a library called Instrument Executable Formats, aptly named `LIEF`. You can add it by typing:

```
pip install
https://github.com/lief-project/LIEF/releases/download/0.7.0/linux_lief-0.7
.0_py3.6.tar.gz
```

Download Gym-malware from `https://github.com/endgameinc/gym-malware`. Move the installed Gym-malware environment to `gym_malware/gym_malware/envs/utils/samples/`.

To check whether you have the samples in the correct directory, type the following:

```
python test_agent_chainer.py
```

The actions available in this environment are as follows:

- append_zero
- append_random_ascii
- append_random_bytes
- remove_signature
- upx_pack
- upx_unpack
- change_section_names_from_list
- change_section_names_to random
- modify_export
- remove_debug
- break_optional_header_checksum

Summary

In this chapter, we continued our journey of learning how to bypass machine learning models. In the previous chapter, we discovered adversarial machine learning; in this continuation, we explored adversarial deep learning and how to fool deep learning networks. We looked at some real-world cases to learn how to escape anti-malware systems by using state of the art techniques. In the next and last chapter, we are going to gain more knowledge, learning how to build robust models.

Questions

1. What are the components of generative adversarial networks?
2. What is the difference between a generator and a discriminator?
3. How can we make sure that the malware adversarial samples are still valid when we are generating them?
4. Do a bit of research, then briefly explain how to detect adversarial samples.
5. What distinguishes reinforcement learning from deep learning?
6. What is the difference between supervised and reinforcement learning?
7. How does an agent learn in reinforcement learning?

Further reading

The following resources include a great deal of information:

- *Explaining and Harnessing Adversarial Samples*: `https://arxiv.org/pdf/1412.6572.pdf`
- *Delving Into Transferable Adversarial Examples and Black Box Attacks*: `https://arxiv.org/pdf/1611.02770.pdf`
- *Foolbox - a Python toolbox to benchmark the robustness of machine learning models*: `https://arxiv.org/pdf/1707.04131.pdf`
- *The Foolbox GitHub*: `https://github.com/bethgelab/foolbox`
- *Generating Adversarial Malware Examples for Black-Box Attacks Based on GAN*: `https://arxiv.org/pdf/1702.05983.pdf`
- *Malware Images: Visualization and Automatic Classification*: `https://arxiv.org/pdf/1702.05983.pdf`
- *SARVAM: Search And RetrieVAl of Malware*: `http://vision.ece.ucsb.edu/sites/vision.ece.ucsb.edu/files/publications/2013_sarvam_ngmad_0.pdf`
- *SigMal: A Static Signal Processing Based Malware Triage*: `http://vision.ece.ucsb.edu/publications/view_abstract.cgi?416`

10
Best Practices for Machine Learning and Feature Engineering

In the previous chapters, we learned about the fundamentals of machine learning, and we learned how to build many different Python projects by using a suite of amazing open source Python libraries. Also, we dove into how to break machine learning models.

This last chapter will help you to build better models by illustrating many tips and best practices for different aspects of your projects.

In this chapter, we will cover the following:

- An in-depth overview of feature engineering in machine learning
- The best practices for machine learning

Technical requirements

You can find the code files for this chapter at https://github.com/PacktPublishing/
Mastering-Machine-Learning-for-Penetration-Testing/tree/master/Chapter10.

Feature engineering in machine learning

Through building and developing all of the projects and prototypes in this book, you have certainly noticed that feature engineering and feature selection are essential to every modern data science product, especially machine learning based projects. According to research, over 50% of the time spent building the model is occupied by cleaning, processing, and selecting the data required to train the model. It is your responsibility to design, represent, and select the features.

Most machine learning algorithms cannot work on raw data. They are not smart enough to do so. Thus, feature engineering is needed, to transform data in its raw status into data that can be understood and consumed by algorithms. Professor Andrew Ng once said:

> *"Coming up with features is difficult, time-consuming, requires expert knowledge.*
> *'Applied machine learning' is basically feature engineering."*

Feature engineering is a process in the data preparation phase, according to the cross-industry standard process for data mining:

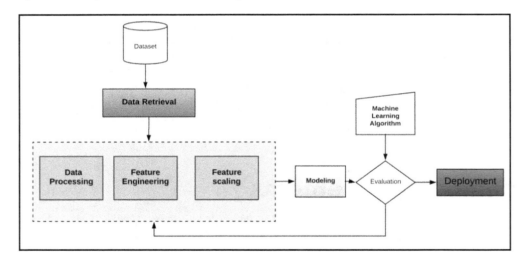

The term **Feature Engineering** itself is not a formally defined term. It groups together all of the tasks for designing features to build intelligent systems. It plays an important role in the system. If you check data science competitions, I bet you have noticed that the competitors all use the same algorithms, but the winners perform the best feature engineering. If you want to enhance your data science and machine learning skills, I highly recommend that you visit and compete at www.kaggle.com:

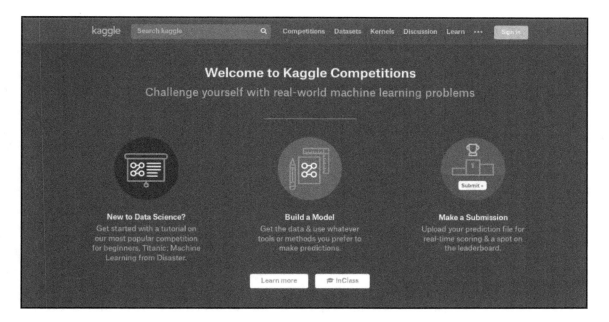

When searching for machine learning resources, you will face many different terminologies. To avoid any confusion, we need to distinguish between feature selection and feature engineering. Feature engineering transforms raw data into suitable features, while feature selection extracts necessary features from the engineered data. Featuring engineering is selecting the subset of all features, without including redundant or irrelevant features.

Feature selection algorithms

To enable the algorithms to train faster, and to reduce the complexity and overfitting of the model, in addition to improving its accuracy, you can use many feature selection algorithms and techniques. We are going to look at three different feature selection methods: filter methods, wrapper methods, and embedded methods. Let's discuss the various methodologies and techniques.

Filter methods

In filter methods, each feature will be assigned a score, computed by different statistical measures. In other words, these methods rank features by considering the relationships between the features and the targets. Filter methods are usually used in the pre-processing phase:

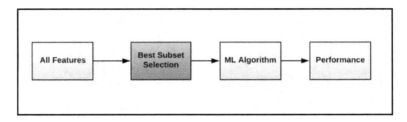

Pearson's correlation

Pearson's correlation is a statistical method used to measure the linear correlation between two variables, x and y. It is ranged between +1 and −1 ; +1 means that there is a positive association. You need to know that x and y should be continuous variables. The formula for Pearson's correlation coefficient is as follows:

$$P_{x,y} = \frac{Cov(X,Y)}{dxdy}$$

Cov is the **covariance,** and dx and dy are the standard deviations of x and y:

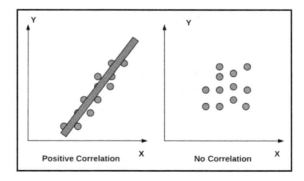

To calculate this using Python, you can use `scipy.stats.pearsonr(x, y)`, from the `scipy` library.

Linear discriminant analysis

In previous chapters, especially in `Chapter 1`, *Introduction to Machine Learning in Pen Testing*, we saw the statistical procedure of **principal component analysis** (**PCA**). **Linear discriminant analysis** (**LDA**) is a dimensionality reduction technique, as well. It is used to find a linear combination of features that separate classes:

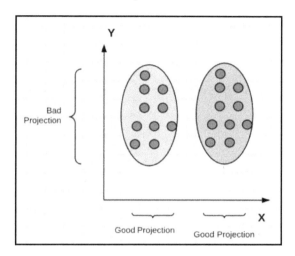

To use LDA with scikit-learn, import it with this line:

```
from sklearn.discriminant_analysis import LinearDiscriminantAnalysis as LDA
```

Use it as follows:

```
sklearn_lda = LDA(n_components=2)
X_lda_sklearn = sklearn_lda.fit_transform(X, y)
```

Analysis of variance

Analysis of variance (**ANOVA**) is like LDA, but it operates using categorical features to check whether the means of several classes are equal, by analyzing the differences between them.

Chi-square

Chi-square is used to determine if a subset data matches a population. The values should be in categories. In other words, the chi-square test is used to check the correlations and associations between the different categories or classes.

The formula for the chi-square test is as follows:

$$X_c^2 = \frac{(O_i - E_i)^2}{E_i}$$

The following is an example of chi-square using scikit-learn, delivered by Jason Brownlee, PhD:

```
import pandas
import numpy
from sklearn.feature_selection import SelectKBest
from sklearn.feature_selection import chi2
# load data
url =
"https://raw.githubusercontent.com/jbrownlee/Datasets/master/pima-indians-d
iabetes.data.csv"
names = ['preg', 'plas', 'pres', 'skin', 'test', 'mass', 'pedi', 'age',
'class']
dataframe = pandas.read_csv(url, names=names)
array = dataframe.values
X = array[:,0:8]
Y = array[:,8]
# feature extraction
test = SelectKBest(score_func=chi2, k=4)
fit = test.fit(X, Y)
# summarize scores
numpy.set_printoptions(precision=3)
print(fit.scores_)
features = fit.transform(X)
# summarize selected features
print(features[0:5,:])
```

The following diagram illustrates the preceding code:

```
                        root@kali: /home/ghost/Chapter10                    ⊖  ⊡  ⊗

 File  Edit  View  Search  Terminal  Help
root@kali:/home/ghost/Chapter10# ls
root@kali:/home/ghost/Chapter10# python
Python 2.7.12+ (default, Aug  4 2016, 20:04:34)
[GCC 6.1.1 20160724] on linux2
Type "help", "copyright", "credits" or "license" for more information.
>>> import pandas
>>> import numpy
>>> from sklearn.feature_selection import SelectKBest
>>> from sklearn.feature_selection import chi2
>>> # load data
... url = "https://raw.githubusercontent.com/jbrownlee/Datasets/master/pima-indians-diabetes.data.cs
v"
>>> names = ['preg', 'plas', 'pres', 'skin', 'test', 'mass', 'pedi', 'age', 'class']
>>> dataframe = pandas.read_csv(url, names=names)
>>> array = dataframe.values
>>> X = array[:,0:8]
>>> Y = array[:,8]
>>> # feature extraction
... test = SelectKBest(score_func=chi2, k=4)
>>> fit = test.fit(X, Y)
>>> # summarize scores
... numpy.set_printoptions(precision=3)
>>> print(fit.scores_)
[ 111.52   1411.887    17.605    53.108  2175.565   127.669      5.393  181.304]
>>> features = fit.transform(X)
>>> # summarize selected features
...
```

Wrapper methods

Wrapper methods are performed by taking subsets and training learning algorithms. Based on the results of the training, we can select the best features for our model. And, as you may have guessed, these methods are computationally very expensive:

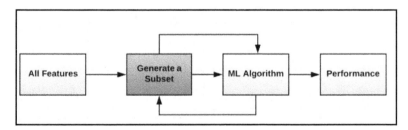

There are many wrapper techniques, including those listed in the following sections.

Forward selection

Forward selection uses searching as a technique for selecting the best features. It is an iterative method. In every iteration, we add more features to improve the model, until we no longer have any further improvements to make:

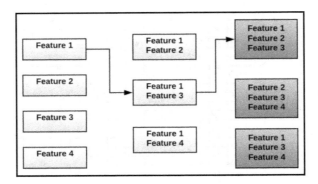

Backward elimination

Backward elimination is like the previous method but, this time, we start with all of the features, and we eliminate some in every iteration until the model stops improving:

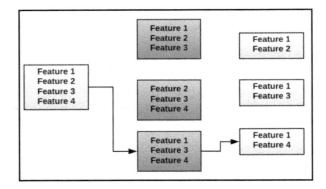

Recursive feature elimination

You can see that recursive feature elimination as a greedy optimization algorithm. This technique is performed by creating models with different subsets and computing the best performing feature, scoring them according to an elimination ranking.

This script is like the previous one, but it uses recursive feature elimination as a feature selection method:

```
from pandas import read_csv
from sklearn.feature_selection import RFE
from sklearn.linear_model import LogisticRegression
# load data
url =
"https://raw.githubusercontent.com/jbrownlee/Datasets/master/pima-indians-d
iabetes.data.csv"
names = ['preg', 'plas', 'pres', 'skin', 'test', 'mass', 'pedi', 'age',
'class']
dataframe = read_csv(url, names=names)
array = dataframe.values
X = array[:,0:8]
Y = array[:,8]
# feature extraction
model = LogisticRegression()
rfe = RFE(model, 3)
fit = rfe.fit(X, Y)
print("Num Features: %d") % fit.n_features_
print("Selected Features: %s") % fit.support_
print("Feature Ranking: %s") % fit.ranking_
```

The following diagram illustrates the preceding code:

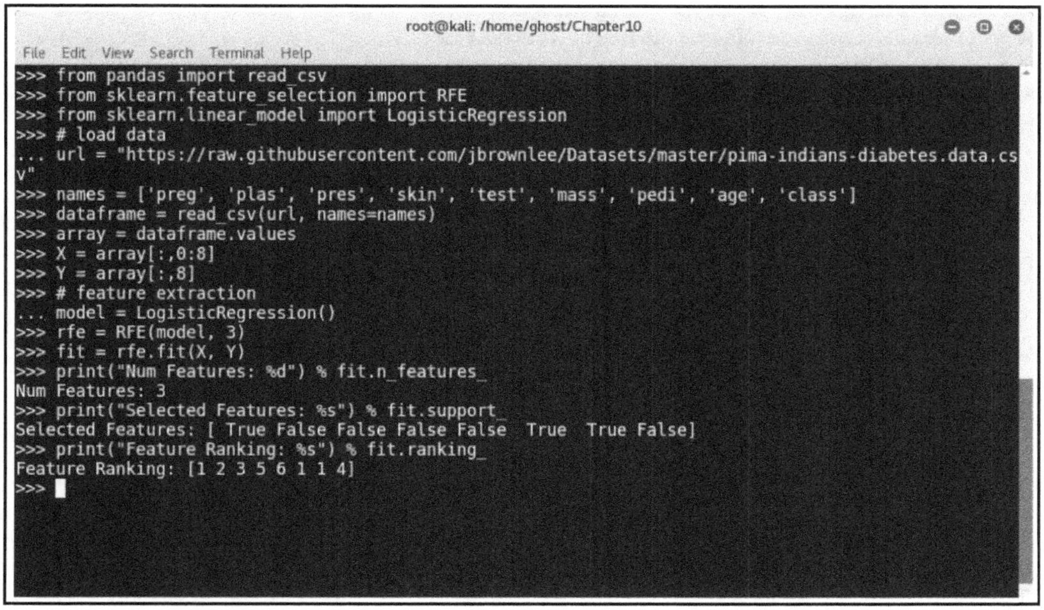

Embedded methods

The main goal of feature selection's embedded method is learning which features are the best in contributing to the accuracy of the machine learning model. They have built-in penalization functions to reduce overfitting:

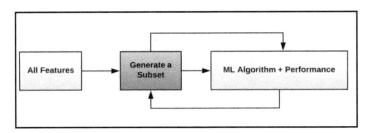

Some of the embedded techniques are listed in the following sections.

Lasso linear regression L1

In statistics, Lasso is a regression analysis method. Lasso linear regression L1 simply adds a penalty equivalent to the absolute value of the magnitude of coefficients. The following is an implementation of the method in Python and sckit-learn:

```
>>> from sklearn.svm import LinearSVC
>>> from sklearn.datasets import load_iris
>>> from sklearn.feature_selection import SelectFromModel
>>> iris = load_iris()
>>> X, y = iris.data, iris.target
>>> X.shape
>>> lsvc = LinearSVC(C=0.01, penalty="l1", dual=False).fit(X, y)
>>> model = SelectFromModel(lsvc, prefit=True)
>>> X_new = model.transform(X)
>>> X_new.shape
```

```
                              ghost@kali: ~/Chapter10                        ● ● ●
File  Edit  View  Search  Terminal  Help
ghost@kali:~/Chapter10$ python
Python 2.7.12+ (default, Aug  4 2016, 20:04:34)
[GCC 6.1.1 20160724] on linux2
Type "help", "copyright", "credits" or "license" for more information.
>>> from sklearn.svm import LinearSVC
>>> from sklearn.datasets import load_iris
>>> from sklearn.feature_selection import SelectFromModel
>>> iris = load_iris()
>>> X, y = iris.data, iris.target
>>> X.shape
(150, 4)
>>> lsvc = LinearSVC(C=0.01, penalty="l1", dual=False).fit(X, y)
>>> model = SelectFromModel(lsvc, prefit=True)
>>> X_new = model.transform(X)
>>> X_new.shape
(150, 3)
>>>
```

Ridge regression L2

The ridge regression L2 method adds a penalty equivalent to the square of the magnitude of coefficients. In other words, it performs an L2 regularization.

Tree-based feature selection

The tree-based feature selection method is used to check and compute feature importance. The following is an example of how we can use the tree-based feature selection technique delivered by the official scikit-learn documentation:

```
>>> from sklearn.ensemble import ExtraTreesClassifier
>>> from sklearn.datasets import load_iris
>>> from sklearn.feature_selection import SelectFromModel
>>> iris = load_iris()
>>> X, y = iris.data, iris.target
>>> X.shape
>>> clf = ExtraTreesClassifier()
>>> clf = clf.fit(X, y)
>>> clf.feature_importances_
>>> model = SelectFromModel(clf, prefit=True)
>>> X_new = model.transform(X)
>>> X_new.shape
```

```
                              ghost@kali: ~/Chapter10
  File  Edit  View  Search  Terminal  Help
  ghost@kali:~/Chapter10$ python
  Python 2.7.12+ (default, Aug  4 2016, 20:04:34)
  [GCC 6.1.1 20160724] on linux2
  Type "help", "copyright", "credits" or "license" for more information.
  >>> from sklearn.ensemble import ExtraTreesClassifier
  >>> from sklearn.datasets import load_iris
  >>> from sklearn.feature_selection import SelectFromModel
  >>> iris = load_iris()
  >>> X, y = iris.data, iris.target
  >>> X.shape
  (150, 4)
  >>> clf = ExtraTreesClassifier()
  >>> clf = clf.fit(X, y)
  >>> clf.feature_importances_
  array([0.17484223, 0.07394988, 0.47573886, 0.27546903])
  >>> model = SelectFromModel(clf, prefit=True)
  >>> X_new = model.transform(X)
  >>> X_new.shape
  (150, 2)
  >>> █
```

As I said previously, feature selection is used in the pre-processing phase, so you can use scikit-learn to build a pipeline, as in the following example:

```
Classifier = Pipeline([
  ('feature_selection', SelectFromModel(<SelectionTechniqueHere>))),
  ('classification', <ClassificationAlgorithmHere>)
])
Classifier.fit(X, y)
```

A great book called *An Introduction to Variable and Feature Selection*, written by Isabelle Guyon and Andre Elisseeff, includes a checklist for better feature selection.

 To learn more about the full checklist, you can browse to `https://machinelearningmastery.com/an-introduction-to-feature-selection/`.

Best practices for machine learning

In the previous sections, we saw how to perform feature engineering to enhance the performance of our machine learning system. Now, we are going to discuss some tips and best practices to build robust intelligent systems. Let's explore some of the best practices in the different aspects of machine learning projects.

Information security datasets

Data is a vital part of every machine learning model. To train models, we need to feed them datasets. While reading the earlier chapters, you will have noticed that to build an accurate and efficient machine learning model, you need a huge volume of data, even after cleaning data. Big companies with great amounts of available data use their internal datasets to build models, but small organizations, like startups, often struggle to acquire such a volume of data. International rules and regulations are making the mission harder because data privacy is an important aspect in information security. Every modern business must protect its users' data. To solve this problem, many institutions and organizations are delivering publicly available datasets, so that others can download them and build their models for educational or commercial use. Some information security datasets are as follows:

- The **Controller Area Network (CAN)** dataset for intrusion detection (OTIDS): http://ocslab.hksecurity.net/Dataset/CAN-intrusion-dataset
- The car-hacking dataset for intrusion detection: http://ocslab.hksecurity.net/Datasets/CAN-intrusion-dataset
- The web-hacking dataset for cyber criminal profiling: http://ocslab.hksecurity.net/Datasets/web-hacking-profiling
- The **API-based malware detection system (APIMDS)** dataset: http://ocslab.hksecurity.net/apimds-dataset
- The intrusion detection evaluation dataset (CICIDS2017): http://www.unb.ca/cic/datasets/ids-2017.html
- The Tor-nonTor dataset: http://www.unb.ca/cic/datasets/tor.html
- The Android adware and general malware dataset: http://www.unb.ca/cic/datasets/android-adware.html

Project Jupyter

The Jupyter Notebook is an open source web application used to create and share coding documents. I highly recommend it, especially for novice data scientists, for many reasons. It will give you the ability to code and visualize output directly. It is great for discovering and playing with data; exploring data is an important step to building machine learning models.

Jupyter's official website is `http://jupyter.org/`:

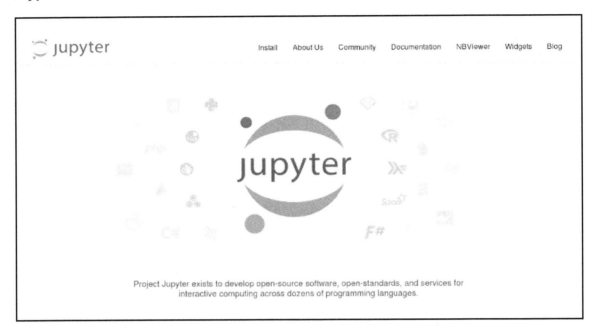

To install it using `pip`, simply type the following:

```
python -m pip install --upgrade pip
python -m pip install jupyter
```

Speed up training with GPUs

As you know, even with good feature engineering, training in machine learning is computationally expensive. The quickest way to train learning algorithms is to use **graphics processing units** (**GPUs**). Generally, though not in all cases, using GPUs is a wise decision for training models. In order to overcome CPU performance bottlenecks, the gather/scatter GPU architecture is best, performing parallel operations to speed up computing.

TensorFlow supports the use of GPUs to train machine learning models. Hence, the devices are represented as strings; following is an example:

```
"/device:GPU:0"  : Your device GPU
"/device:GPU:1"  : 2nd GPU device on your Machine
```

To use a GPU device in TensorFlow, you can add the following line:

```
with tf.device('/device:GPU:0'):
    <What to Do Here>
```

You can use a single GPU or multiple GPUs. Don't forget to install the CUDA toolkit, by using the following commands:

```
Wget
"http://developer.download.nvidia.com/compute/cuda/repos/ubuntu1604/x86_64/
cuda-repo-ubuntu1604_8.0.44-1_amd64.deb"

sudo dpkg -i cuda-repo-ubuntu1604_8.0.44-1_amd64.deb

sudo apt-get update

sudo apt-get install cuda
```

Install cuDNN as follows:

```
sudo tar -xvf cudnn-8.0-linux-x64-v5.1.tgz -C /usr/local

export PATH=/usr/local/cuda/bin:$PATH

export
LD_LIBRARY_PATH="$LD_LIBRARY_PATH:/usr/local/cuda/lib64:/usr/local/cuda/ext
ras/CUPTI/lib64"
export CUDA_HOME=/usr/local/cuda
```

Selecting models and learning curves

To improve the performance of machine learning models, there are many hyper parameters to adjust. The more data that is used, the more errors that can happen. To work on these parameters, there is a method called `GridSearchCV`. It performs searches on predefined parameter values, through iterations. `GridSearchCV` uses the `score()` function, by default. To use it in scikit-learn, import it by using this line:

```
from sklearn.grid_search import GridSearchCV
```

Learning curves are used to understand the performance of a machine learning model. To use a learning curve in scikit-learn, import it to your Python project, as follows:

```
from sklearn.learning_curve import learning_curve
```

Machine learning architecture

In the real world, data scientists do not find data to be as clean as the publicly available datasets. Real world data is stored by different means, and the data itself is shaped in different categories. Thus, machine learning practitioners need to build their own systems and pipelines to achieve their goals and train the models. A typical machine learning project respects the following architecture:

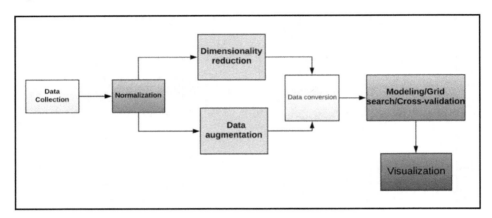

Coding

Good coding skills are very important to data science and machine learning. In addition to using effective linear algebra, statistics, and mathematics, data scientists should learn how to code properly. As a data scientist, you can choose from many programming languages, like Python, R, Java, and so on.

Respecting coding's best practices is very helpful and highly recommended. Writing elegant, clean, and understandable code can be done through these tips:

- Comments are very important to understandable code. So, don't forget to comment your code, all of the time.
- Choose the right names for variables, functions, methods, packages, and modules.
- Use four spaces per indentation level.
- Structure your repository properly.
- Follow common style guidelines.

If you use Python, you can follow this great aphorism, called the *The Zen of Python*, written by the legend, Tim Peters:

> *"Beautiful is better than ugly.*
> *Explicit is better than implicit.*
> *Simple is better than complex.*
> *Complex is better than complicated.*
> *Flat is better than nested.*
> *Sparse is better than dense.*
> *Readability counts.*
> *Special cases aren't special enough to break the rules.*
> *Although practicality beats purity.*
> *Errors should never pass silently.*
> *Unless explicitly silenced.*
> *In the face of ambiguity, refuse the temptation to guess.*
> *There should be one-- and preferably only one --obvious way to do it.*
> *Although that way may not be obvious at first unless you're Dutch.*
> *Now is better than never.*
> *Although never is often better than *right* now.*
> *If the implementation is hard to explain, it's a bad idea.*
> *If the implementation is easy to explain, it may be a good idea.*
> *Namespaces are one honking great idea -- let's do more of those!"*

Data handling

Good data handling leads to successfully building machine learning projects. After loading a dataset, please make sure that all of the data has loaded properly, and that the reading process is performing correctly. After performing any operation on the dataset, check over the resulting dataset.

Business contexts

An intelligent system is highly connected to business aspects because, after all, you are using data science and machine learning to solve a business issue or to build a commercial product, or for getting useful insights from the data that is acquired, to make good decisions. Identifying the right problems and asking the right questions are important when building your machine learning model, in order to solve business issues.

Summary

This book was a practical guide for learning how to build machine learning projects to defend against cyber threats and malicious activities, using open source libraries, Python, and a set of open source projects. We didn't stop there; we also showed you how to attack those models using adversarial machine learning. Through that, you acquired a set of skills to analyze data, build defensive systems, and break next-generation safeguards. We finished the book by discussing many points to help you build better models.

Questions

1. What is the difference between feature engineering and feature selection?
2. What is the difference between principal component analysis (PCA) and feature selection?
3. How can we encode features like dates and hours?
4. Why it is useful to print out training and testing accuracy?
5. How can we deploy a machine learning model and use it in a product?
6. Why does feature engineering take much more time than other steps?
7. What is the role of a dummy variable?

Further reading

Papers and slides:

- *Feature Engineering - Knowledge Discovery and Data Mining 1*, by Roman Kern: http://kti.tugraz.at/staff/denis/courses/kddm1/featureengineering.pdf
- *Feature Engineering and Selection* (https://people.eecs.berkeley.edu/~jordan/courses/294-fall09/lectures/feature/slides.pdf) *- CS 294: Practical Machine Learning*, Berkeley: https://people.eecs.berkeley.edu/~jordan/courses/294-fall09/lectures/feature/
- *Feature Engineering* by Leon Bottou, Princeton: http://www.cs.princeton.edu/courses/archive/spring10/cos424/slides/18-feat.pdf

Blog posts:

- *Discover Feature Engineering - How to Engineer Features and How to Get Good at It:* https://machinelearningmastery.com/discover-feature-engineering-how-to-engineer-features-and-how-to-get-good-at-it/
- *Machine Learning Mastery:* https://machinelearningmastery.com/start-here/

Books:

- *Feature Extraction, Construction, and Selection: A Data Mining Perspective:* https://www.amazon.com/dp/0792381963?tag=inspiredalgor-20
- *Feature Extraction: Foundations and Applications:* https://www.amazon.com/dp/3540354875?tag=inspiredalgor-20
- *Feature Extraction and Image Processing for Computer Vision, Third Edition:* https://www.amazon.com/dp/0123965497?tag=inspiredalgor-20

Assessments

Chapter 1 – Introduction to Machine Learning in Pentesting

1. Although machine learning is an interesting concept, there are limited business applications in which it is useful.

   False

2. Machine learning applications are too complex to run in the cloud.

   False

3. For two runs of k-means clustering, is it expected to get the same clustering results?

   No

4. Predictive models having target attributes with discrete values can be termed as:

   Classification models

5. Which of the following techniques perform operations similar to dropouts in a neural network?

   Bagging

6. Which architecture of a neural network would be best suited for solving an image recognition problem?

   A convolutional neural network

7. How does deep learning differ from conventional machine learning?

   Deep learning algorithms can handle more data and run with less supervision from data scientists.

8. Which of the following is a technique frequently used in machine learning projects?

   All of the above

Chapter 2 – Phishing Domain Detection

1. The following are some text-cleaning tasks to perform:
   - Clean your texts of stopwords, digits, and punctuation marks.
   - Perform lemmatization.
2. Create a word dictionary, including their frequencies.
3. Remove the non-words from the dictionary.
4. Extract the features from the data.

   Check `Chapter2-Practice` folder for the answers: `https://github.com/PacktPublishing/Mastering-Machine-Learning-for-Penetration-Testing/tree/master/Chapter%202/Chaptre2-Practice`.

5. Prepare the feature vectors and their labels.

```
train_labels = np.zeros(702)
train_labels[351:701] = 1
train_matrix = extract_features(train_dir)
```

6. Train the model with a linear support vector machine classifier.

```
model = LinearSVC()
model.fit(train_matrix,train_labels)
```

7. Print out the confusion matrix of your model.

```
result = model.predict(test_matrix)
print (confusion_matrix(test_labels,result))
```

Chapter 3 – Malware Detection with API Calls and PE Headers

1. Load the dataset using the pandas python library, and this time, add the low_memory=False parameter. Search for what that parameter does.

   ```
   df = pd.read_csv(file_name, low_memory=False)
   ```

2. Prepare the data that will be used for training.

   ```
   original_headers = list(df.columns.values)
   total_data = df[original_headers[:-1]]
   total_data = total_data.as_matrix()
   target_strings = df[original_headers[-1]]
   ```

3. Split the data with the test_size=0.33 parameter.

   ```
   train, test, target_train, target_test =
   train_test_split(total_data, target_strings, test_size=0.33,
   random_state=int(time.time()))
   ```

4. Create a set of classifiers that contains DecisionTreeClassifier(), RandomForestClassifier(n_estimators=100), and AdaBoostClassifier():

   ```
   classifiers = [
   RandomForestClassifier(n_estimators=100),
   DecisionTreeClassifier(),
   AdaBoostClassifier()]
   ```

5. What is an AdaBoostClassifier()?

   An AdaBoost classifier is a meta-estimator that begins by fitting a classifier on the original dataset and then fits additional copies of the classifier on the same dataset.

6. Train the model using the three classifiers and print out the metrics of every classifier.

   Check the Chapter3-Practice folder for the solution: https://github.com/PacktPublishing/Mastering-Machine-Learning-for-Penetration-Testing/tree/master/Chapter%203/Chapter3-Practice.

Chapter 4 – Malware Detection with Deep Learning

1. What is the difference between MLP networks and deep learning networks?

   Deep networks are already multi-layer perceptron networks but with at least three hidden layers.

2. Why DL recently is taking off?

   Because we have access to a lot more computational power and data.

3. Why do we need to iterate multiple times through different models?

   Because nobody can always find the best model or hyperparameter without iterations.

4. What type of DL needed to translate English to French language?

   Recurrent Neural Network (RNN)

5. Why malware visualization is a good method to classify malware?

   Because we can use state-of-the-art image recognition to build malware classifiers.

6. What is the role of an activation function?

   It defines the output of a given node. In other words, it converts an input signal of a node in an A-NN to an output signal.

7. Can you mention three DL architectures?
   - **Convolutional Neural Networks (CNNs)**
   - **Recurrent Neural Networks (RNNs)**
   - **Long/Short Term Memory Networks (LSTMs)**

Chapter 5 – Botnet Detection with Machine Learning

As we did after every chapter, we are going to give you the opportunity to practice what you have learned and evaluate your skills. This chapter's GitHub repository contains a link to botnet traffic dataset in the practice folder at `https://github.com/PacktPublishing/Mastering-Machine-Learning-for-Penetration-Testing/tree/master/Chapter5`:

1. Download the dataset and load it with the pandas library
2. Select the suitable features
3. Identify the training and testing sets, then export them into a `.pickle` file
4. Load the `.pickle` file
5. Use the same code blocks of `Chapter 5`, *Botnet Detection with Machine Learning*.

    Import a support vector machine classifier:

    ```
    from sklearn.svm import *
    ```

    Train the SVM model:

    ```
    clf= SVC(kernel='rbf')
    clf.fit(Xdata, Ydata)
    ```

    Print out the accuracy of the built model:

    ```
    Score = clf.score(XdataT,YdataT)
    print ("The Score of the SVM Classifier is", Score * 100)
    ```

Chapter 6 – Machine Learning in Anomaly Detection Systems

1. What is an anomaly?

    An anomaly is something that deviates from what is standard, normal, or expected.

2. What is a Markov chain?

   A Markov chain, or what we call a Markov process, is a stochastic model used for any random system that change its states according to fixed probabilities.

3. What are Hidden Markov models?

   The Hidden Markov Model is a Markov process where we are unable to directly observe the state of the system. Each state has a fixed probability of **emitting**. The main goal of an HMM model or classifier is assigning a label to a family of sequences, which means linking a sequence of observations to a sequence of labels.

4. How can we detect anomalies with Hidden Markov models?

   According to the Hidden Markov Model definition, we can use it to discriminate between normal and abnormal behavior of network traffic.

5. What's the difference between time series anomaly detection and other types of anomaly detection?

   Time series are values obtained at successive times, often with equal intervals between them. In time series anomaly detection, we are detecting anomalies in sequences of data points being recorded at specific times. In most other detection methods, we are using techniques such as the graph-based technique.

6. What's the difference between supervised and unsupervised machine learning anomaly detection?

   The difference between the two models is based on the machine learning algorithms used. For example, in supervised machine learning anomaly detection, we can use classification; while in unsupervised machine learning anomaly detection, we can use clustering.

Chapter 7 – Detecting Advanced Persistent Threats

1. Which of the following is not a step in the cyber kill chain?

    (a) Scanning

2. Which of the following options is not a node of the diamond model of intrusion analysis?

    (c) Procedures

3. How many parts are needed in a Logstash configuration file?

    (b) 3

4. In ElasticSearch, what is indexing?

    (a) The process of storing data in an index

5. In Elasticsearch, what is a node?

    (a) An instance of Elasticsearch

6. In Elasticsearch, what is a shard?

    (c) Shared resources (RAM, vCPU)

7. Does Elasticsearch have a schema?

    (a) Yes

Chapter 8 – Evading Intrusion Detection Systems with Adversarial Machine Learning

1. Can you briefly explain why overtraining a machine learning model is not a good idea?

   By overtraining a machine learning model by training data too well, we train the model in a way that negatively impacts the performance of the model on new data. It is also referred to as *overfitting*.

2. What is the difference between overfitting and underfitting?

   Overfitting refers to overtraining the model, while underfitting refers to a model that can neither model the training data nor generalize to new data.

3. What is the difference between an evasion and poisoning attack?

   In an evasion adversarial attack, the attacker try many different samples to identify a learning pattern to bypass it; while in poisoning attacks, the attacker poisons the model in the training phase.

4. How does adversarial clustering work?

   Adversarial clustering occurs when the attackers manipulates the input data (adding small percentage of attack samples) so the newly added sample can hide within the existing clusters.

5. What type of adversarial attack is used to avoid the intrusion detection system?

   The attack used in the demonstration is called the **Jacobian-based Saliency Map** attack.

6. Is the preceding attack an evasion or poisoning attack?

   It is a poisoning adversarial attack.

Chapter 9 – Bypass Machine Learning Malware Detectors

1. What are the components of generative adversarial networks?

   The two main components of a generative adversarial network are the generator and the discriminator.

2. What is the difference between a generator and a discriminator?

   The generator takes latent samples as input. They are randomly generated numbers and they are trained to generate images, while the discriminator is simply a classifier trained with supervised learning techniques to check whether the image is real (1) or fake (0).

3. How can we make sure that the malware adversarial samples are still valid when we are generating them?

   To avoid invalid samples, we can use a Sandbox/Oracle.

4. Do a bit of research, then briefly explain how to detect adversarial samples

   To detect adversarial samples, we can remove the noise by using binary thresholding.

5. What distinguishes reinforcement learning from deep learning?

   Reinforcement learning learns how to maximize a reward function by exploring the actions available from certain states, while deep learning learns from examples it has been shown.

6. What is the difference between supervised and reinforcement learning?

   In supervised learning, given input data X and labels Y we are learning a function $f: X \rightarrow Y$ that maps X to Y. In reinforcement learning, the agents are getting smarter after number of experiences.

7. How does an agent learn in reinforcement learning?

In reinforcement learning, the agent learns by interacting with an environment based on a reward function to optimize its performance.

Chapter 10 – Best Practices for Machine Learning and Feature Engineering

1. What is the difference between feature engineering and feature selection?

   Feature selection is a part of feature engineering.

2. What is the difference between **principal component analysis (PCA)** and feature selection?

   Feature selection takes the dataset and gives us the best set of features, while PCA is a dimensionality reduction method.

3. How can we encode features like dates and hours?

   One of the techniques is adding the (sine, cosine) transformation of the time of day variable.

4. Why it is useful to print out training and testing accuracy?

   It is useful to detect overfitting by comparing the two metrics.

5. How can we deploy a machine learning model and use it in a product?

   There are many ways to take a machine learning model to production, such as web services and containerization depending on your model (Online, offline? Deep learning, SVM, Naive Bayes?).

6. Why does feature engineering take much more time than other steps?

   Because analyzing, cleaning, and processing features takes more time than building the model.

7. What is the role of a dummy variable?

   A dummy variable is a numerical variable used in regression analysis to represent subgroups of the sample in your study. In research design, a dummy variable is often used to distinguish between different treatment groups.

Other Books You May Enjoy

If you enjoyed this book, you may be interested in these other books by Packt:

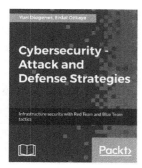

Cybersecurity – Attack and Defense Strategies
Yuri Diogenes, Erdal Ozkaya

ISBN: 978-1-78847-529-7

- Learn the importance of having a solid foundation for your security posture
- Understand the attack strategy using cyber security kill chain
- Learn how to enhance your defense strategy by improving your security policies, hardening your network, implementing active sensors, and leveraging threat intelligence
- Learn how to perform an incident investigation
- Get an in-depth understanding of the recovery process
- Understand continuous security monitoring and how to implement a vulnerability management strategy
- Learn how to perform log analysis to identify suspicious activities

Machine Learning Solutions
Jalaj Thanaki

ISBN: 978-1-78839-004-0

- Select the right algorithm to derive the best solution in ML domains
- Perform predictive analysis efficiently using ML algorithms
- Predict stock prices using the stock index value
- Perform customer analytics for an e-commerce platform
- Build recommendation engines for various domains
- Build NLP applications for the health domain
- Build language generation applications using different NLP techniques
- Build computer vision applications such as facial emotion recognition

Mastering Metasploit - Third Edition
Nipun Jaswal

ISBN: 978-1-78899-061-5

- Develop advanced and sophisticated auxiliary modules
- Port exploits from PERL, Python, and many more programming languages
- Test services such as databases, SCADA, and many more
- Attack the client side with highly advanced techniques
- Test mobile and tablet devices with Metasploit
- Bypass modern protections such as an AntiVirus and IDS with Metasploit
- Simulate attacks on web servers and systems with Armitage GUI
- Script attacks in Armitage using CORTANA scripting

Kali Linux - An Ethical Hacker's Cookbook
Himanshu Sharma

ISBN: 978-1-78712-182-9

- Installing, setting up and customizing Kali for pentesting on multiple platforms
- Pentesting routers and embedded devices
- Bug hunting 2017
- Pwning and escalating through corporate network
- Buffer overflows 101
- Auditing wireless networks
- Fiddling around with software-defned radio
- Hacking on the run with NetHunter
- Writing good quality reports

Leave a review - let other readers know what you think

Please share your thoughts on this book with others by leaving a review on the site that you bought it from. If you purchased the book from Amazon, please leave us an honest review on this book's Amazon page. This is vital so that other potential readers can see and use your unbiased opinion to make purchasing decisions, we can understand what our customers think about our products, and our authors can see your feedback on the title that they have worked with Packt to create. It will only take a few minutes of your time, but is valuable to other potential customers, our authors, and Packt. Thank you!

Index